D1707277

*Mama*
*Doesn't*
*Live Here*
*Anymore*

# Mama Doesn't Live Here Anymore

## Judy Sullivan

*A*

ARTHUR FIELDS BOOKS, INC. NEW YORK, 1974

Copyright 1974 © by Judy Sullivan
All rights reserved. Printed in the U.S.A.
First Edition

10 9 8 7 6 5 4 3 2 1

No part of this publication may be reproduced or transmitted
in any form or by any means, electronic or mechanical, including
photocopy, recording, or any information storage and retrieval
system now known or to be invented, without permission in writing
from the publisher, except by a reviewer who wishes to quote brief
passages in connection with a review written for inclusion in a
magazine, newspaper or broadcast.

Published simultaneously in Canada by Clarke, Irwin & Company
Limited, Toronto and Vancouver
ISBN: 0-525-63011-2
Library of Congress Catalog Card Number: 73-18889

*Hanoi Journals* copyright © 1968 by Susan Santag is quoted
here with the permission of Farrar, Straus & Giroux, Inc.

*For Kathleen and all my other Sisters*

*Mama*
*Doesn't*
*Live Here*
*Anymore*

# Prologue

Three years ago I left my husband and my daughter in the small college town of Emporia, Kansas, and came to New York to find my life. On a cold and rainy morning two years later, I opened the *Times* and saw my picture, two columns wide and half a page long, staring me back in the face. It was there because the media had decided I was a "runaway wife"; it wasn't the first newspaper article about me, and special only because it was *The New York Times*. I did that interview and others, and will continue to do them, and have written this book, out of a sense of obligation to other women who have also left their families, or who might be thinking about it. There are more of us every day.

What I left behind represented for me, and for most women of my age and class, a living-out of the American dream—a loving husband, a happy and well-behaved child, a beautiful home, an interesting career. Togetherness and success; happiness and fulfillment. But I gave up the twelve-room house in Emporia's "nicest" neighborhood, two cars and a boat, years of carefully acquired and inherited household goods, and most of my wardrobe. I came to New York alone with what I could carry in a small straw trunk and one valise, looking like a Chinese missionary—with a few dollars I'd managed to save, mostly from the sale of my share of the household, and with a very naive idea of what my life would be for the rest of it.

I knew I had hurt a number of people, radically rearranged their lives forever.

I knew I was taking the greatest risk of my life. I had never even heard of another woman, then, who had done such a thing, though certainly it's something men do every day. There were male "runaways" in my own family; my father and mother were divorced when I was eleven, leaving my brother and me with our mother; and that same brother, when he grew up, left not one but two families. Are only women bolters rare enough to be news?

Often these newspaper accounts simplified and sensationalized the facts. I didn't "run away," which sounds childish and irresponsible; I didn't even "drop out." I prepared for my departure very carefully, over a long period of time. I announced my decision to the people most directly involved a full nine months before I carried it out, and when I did leave, everybody knew exactly where I went.

Because leaving home was such a cataclysmic thing, because it was so profoundly personal, because it was such an intimate upheaval, it was hard to get detached enough about the whole business to be able to deliver up for concerned relatives and friends, much less the media, some sort of easily digestible explanation. The very fact that I was not only thinking but actually *doing* what most people consider unthinkable was enough to confuse the issue probably for good and all. I've never felt quite comfortable about making my private life public; but other women who have what I always called the "running blues" need to know they aren't alone.

The immediate assumption, on the part of a lot of people, was that I had to be crazy, or at the very least, selfish and heartless beyond belief, to have given up so much, to have caused so much grief. I knew that I wasn't crazy; the problem was that I had just made an awful discovery. I suddenly saw that my marriage was just that—mine. My husband had another one, and it was quite different. By the examples of our parents, by the exigencies of our life together for fifteen years, somehow an iron-clad nonconscious marriage contract had been drawn. To live up to that contract, I would have to be somebody I was not. Once the terms of that contract came clear to me, I couldn't ignore it, something had to be done.

I did it.

Anne, a colleague from the university where I used to teach, came to see me last year, when she and her husband and children were in New York for a visit. We had been good friends. We had shared an office for several years, and the same secretary, and the same baby sitters; she lived only a block away from me, in the same neighborhood, in a house built by the same architect who built my house. We knew many of the same people, and she had sponsored my admission into the most exclusive women's club in Emporia.

She had been shaken when I told her I intended to leave John and Kathleen and come to New York. I think she thought she knew me better, that we were more alike, and I'm quite sure she never dreamed I'd do anything like that.

We still thought of each other as friends—and we had dinner together that night in New York.

She met a few of my new friends, scrutinized the large one-room apartment I was lucky to get, with its makeshift furniture and bookshelves, its open kitchen. This was a totally different world from the one she and I had inhabited in Emporia. She seemed sad, but nervous, even threatened by it all. Perhaps she was thinking: *Here's this woman whom I liked, whom I thought I liked, thought I knew, who is very much like me, and she's saying that all the values I thought we held in common are worthless. Is everything I worked so hard for not really worth having?*

She was distant, cool, but still was obviously concerned about me, and wanted to know what I was doing. She was too polite to ask if I regretted what I'd done and too well-bred to probe into my private life, as other people often do. Our talk drifted into the genteel exchanges I had had so many times in Emporia, talk that kept us from knowing either ourselves or each other.

I couldn't blame her. She was just trying to understand—just as so many others had tried to understand.

Just trying to explain to my husband and my daughter why I had to leave, loving them all the while, was as close to impossible as anything I've ever attempted.

Why did I leave Kathleen?

How *could* I leave my own daughter?

It is, as they say, a long story—one that begins with an elaborate Texas wedding; no, before that—in Hamilton, Texas, in attitudes that were always part of the life I knew. No doubt it begins farther back than that, far beyond the particulars of my life; the problem is fundamental to the relationship of all men and women.

But Hamilton will have to do for a start. *Hamilton?*

Look for it on the map. It's a dot, surrounded by a few other dots with names like Pottsville, Cranfills Gap, Gustine, and Priddy; a hundred miles west of Waco and even farther from Fort Worth, Dallas, and Austin, the nearest cities. It was a small, cloistered, old-fashioned place, and had a rigid social code when I lived there in the 1940s and 50s. My family happened to be "old family," so I was brought up to be a charming southern belle. The training was subtle but rigorous, so rigorous I still feel some of that old person in me, just as, at times, I still find echoes of the Kansas housewife.

If I didn't live up to Hamilton expectations, it's not because the world of Hamilton didn't try hard enough. It did. So did I. For a great many years—years that did not lack their joys and pleasures.

Though I left my old life with a large set of reasons why, the list has changed and grown and clarified over these past three years, and this writing has accelerated that process. It has been a difficult book to write. I will never be satisfied with it, really, because it doesn't do justice either to the people or to the events. People I love very much, who have been important to me, will find themselves mentioned barely or not at all. Others will think the picture of them is harsh, even bitter. I don't mean for it to be. We all did what we were expected to do, what society had said we ought. We all did that for a long time.

Then I stopped.

# One

## Miz Lady

# 1

## "Hamiltone-town, We're Going to Ham-il-ton!"

"A wedding of unusual beauty and impressive dignity," the Hamilton *Herald-Record* reported on March 23, 1934, "was solemnized at the home in this city of E. A. Perry, grandfather of the bride, on March 17, at ten o'clock in the morning when Miss Mary Lou Sikes was given in holy marriage to Lieutenant Jesse Harrison Turner, of the 358th U.S. Infantry, Fort Sam Houston . . . For the occasion the entire lower floor of the stately Perry home was thrown en suite with floral adornment that was tasteful, artistic and truly beautiful . . . The marriage of Miss Mary Lou Sikes was of unusual interest universally in Hamilton and the county. She was born in this city, and is a descendant of two of Hamilton County's oldest and most prominently known pioneer families, the Perrys and the Clarks . . . She has a kind heart and a bright and ready smile that endears her to every age and class of people . . . The groom was born in Meridian, Texas . . . He graduated from Virginia Military Institute at Lexington . . . He is held in highest esteem wherever he is known, and gives the impression that he is able to fully safeguard the happiness of the adorable young girl whom he honors with his name and to whom he trusts his future welfare and joy in living . . ."

The young couple that Miss Clara Linton described in her inimitable fashion were my parents. And they seemed to me, when I was a small child, to be all that she wrote and more. My mother was beautiful and vivacious, with so much charm that everyone who met her loved her immediately. My father was handsome and elegantly reserved, a military man to the core, even after he resigned his commission and went back to civil engineering to help his stepfather's Depression-floundering construction business in Abilene, Texas.

They moved to Abilene, where my father had grown up, before I was born in 1936. I can remember our white frame house; the yellow roses on the wallpaper of my bedroom; the kitchen table where I ate except on special occasions when I was allowed to join the grownups; my mother's dressing table where I used to watch her brush her long shiny hair and then coil it on the back of her neck, tucking in the gardenia my father always brought her to wear to the country club dances. I remember her soft, long dresses, the flowers and perfumes, her delighted excitement before a party. I remember all the pretty shoes, of pastel suede, elegant hats and gloves, the closet full of flower-colored dresses of crepe and voile, smelling like Mama. The closet was one of my favorite places, dressing up and playing "Miz Lady," my favorite game.

My grandfather died before his construction business did. No one was building anything in Abilene in the late 1930s, so my father, whom I called Pappy, took me to work with him often. I liked to sit with him at the high blueprint table, while he drew pictures for me with the sure, bold hand of a draftsman. He also taught me how to box and how to present arms with his saber; the saber was bigger than I was. And he told me stories about VMI, when he was a "Brother Rat." Could I go to VMI? Could I be a Brother Rat? It sounded even more exciting than Miz Lady. No, that was for my brother, who would be along one of these days.

I would be Miz Lady.

My mother's sister, my Aunt Tink, who was as pretty as Mama but taller, slenderer, was a frequent visitor. Her daughter, my cousin Pamela, was just nine months my junior. Pam was full of mischief and invention, and our games together often got us into trouble. Once we were left with a maid more interested in *True Confession* magazines than us; she read contentedly while we painted each other from head to foot with crimson nail polish. I can still remember how the polish remover stung when the grownups came home and, laughing even as they fussed at us, restored us to our natural state and put us to bed.

Mama and Aunt Tink always had more fun than anybody. Theirs was an Irish family, a southern family, preferring each other's company over anyone else's—always laughing and singing, drinking beer and telling funny stories when they were together. It was so much more fun to go back to Hamilton for a family reunion than it was to visit my Abilene grandmother's sad, dark house where I was often left to spend Saturday night and be taken to church the next morning. Mam-Ma Oates, my father's mother, was twice widowed and lived alone in the big brick house her contractor husband had built for her in better times. It always smelled of Lysol. There was never anything to eat but things that were good for you—like milquetoast and cream of wheat. The living room was blighted with a full-scale reproduction of Millet's "The Gleaners"—dark, heavy, depressing.

There were only two really interesting things in that house for a little girl: one was my grandmother's big mahogany secretary, with its compartments and tiny drawers inside the folded-up lid. I wasn't allowed to touch it. The other was her bathroom. Old Daddy Oates had gotten all lavender fixtures for it. In those days, such a thing was very rare, indeed—I'd certainly never seen anything but white bathrooms in all my young life. So my big treat there was taking a bath in the lavendar tub.

But, oh, my other grandmother's house in Hamilton! To go there was a glory and an expedition, setting out in the big old car and driving for hours; often Pam came along with us, the two of us bouncing up and down on the back seat and singing until everybody was ready to throttle us: *Hamiltone-town, Hamiltone-town, we're going to Hamil-ton!*

Abilene was West Texas—flat, windy, and ravaged with dust storms; Hamilton, two hundred miles away in a valley in central Texas, seemed like another world. It was situated at the juncture of two highways: to the south were rolling prairie and grass lands, with few trees except along the river beds, and in drought years the pastures grew dry and dusty; to the north were stands of scrub-oak timber.

But it was as a *world* that Hamilton was most different.

It was old-fashioned and self-contained. Mama and Aunt Tink loved to tell us stories of the good times they'd had growing up there, picnics among the pecan trees beside the Leon River, the dances at the country club my great-grandfather Perry built and named after himself, the mischief they'd gotten into in my great-grandmother Perry's wine cellar, how my grandmother always dressed up as Santa Claus and crammed herself up the chimney so she could pop out and fool them all. None of them ever knew it was really Mam-Ma, not even my Uncle Edben, who next to our daddies we knew had to be the smartest man in the world.

One of our favorite stories was the one about Edben's horse. It seemed he'd wanted a horse for ever so long and finally, when he was about eight years old and sick with the croup, Old Daddy brought one home for him. Edben's bed was moved so he could watch his horse from the window. It wasn't much of a horse, but Edben loved him and could hardly wait until he was well enough to ride. He named him Booger Red and watched him every day. One morning, when poor little sick Edben woke up and looked out the window, there was Booger Red, leaning up against the side of the barn and deader than a doornail.

Aunt Tink told the story, stretching it out forever, with a lot of eye-rolling and hand-wringing to make it plenty melodramatic; and it never failed to make us laugh until our sides hurt, though, to save my neck, I still can't understand what's so funny about a sick little boy crying for his dead horse. It had to be Aunt Tink's rendition of it—she was the best storyteller of them all.

We were the first grandchildren, Pam and I, and we were spoiled outrageously. On every trip back to Hamilton we were dressed up, often in matching outfits that Mama or Mam-Ma made for us, and taken visiting to all the old friends and myriad assorted relations. We were passed around from family to family, from house to house, so that not until I was grown did I know precisely who was actually kin; until I was twelve I thought that one of

John's aunts was mine as well—she and my mother had been best friends since infancy and I'd always called her Aunt Nell.

When all the friends and relations had been visited, we would be taken to town and paraded around the square. And everywhere we went, dressed in our matching finery, scrubbed, combed, and beribboned, we were ooohed and aaaahed over, and people would just have fits over us.

If *pretty* was what we were supposed to be, we were a giant success.

Pam, with her almost snow-white hair and china-blue eyes, was usually dressed in blue; my golden hair and brown eyes made pink my color. We said appropriately "cute" things, and Miss Clara Linton delightedly made note of them, and us, in her society column in the *Herald*.

Pam and I were the newest members of one of Hamilton's oldest families—something I became aware of very early and wasn't allowed to forget. Little was said directly, but the message that we were different from other folks was very clear. It usually went something like: "Well, other people may do such-and-such, but *we* don't!" Such-and-such could be anything considered either common or simply improper—going bowling, riding motorcycles, living in a trailer, socializing with Negroes or with ladies smoking in the street.

There was always a great deal of kissing in the family. My Uncle Edben kissed his father if he hadn't seen him for a while. And everyone always kissed the ladies and the children.

The husbands, though different from each other in many respects, were all alike in one. They were uxorious in the particular manner of southern gentlemen: they

doted on their wives. Wives were always called by something other than their names—"darlin'," "precious,"
"baby," or "girlwife." My father called my mother "pet."
The gentlemen fussed over their wives with such tender
regard it would have been absurd had it not seemed so sin-
cere. Chairs were always fetched and carefully positioned
out of the sun, in the breeze or away from it. Fans were
brought (the round paper ones with stick handles and an
advertisement for Riley's Funeral Home), drinks mixed
and delivered, elaborate compliments paid.

"I've never seen baby look as pretty as she does tonight,
now wouldn't you all agree? She's as slender and lovely as
the day she was my little girl bride, now don't you all
think so?"

Everyone would agree, and baby would smile and fan
herself demurely, whooshing whiffs of sachet all about her
in the summer night air.

That was the way Ladies were treated by their husbands. The way the husbands were treated by their wives
was another, more complicated, matter.

When the husbands were not around, or "underfoot," as
they would say, the wives would tell stories and laugh
about how helpless they were, these all-powerful men.
How the slightest little cold could lay them flatter than a
flitter, and how it was a good thing they never had the
cramps; they'd die for sure. Yet always these remarks
would be modified in the end: "But Lord knows, he's the
sweetest man in the world; he hasn't a selfish bone in his
body."

Aunt Tink used to tell stories about how she and Uncle
Bill fought when they were first married. That she'd gotten so mad at him because he never put his dirty clothes in
the hamper, she took to hiding them under the bed until

he didn't have anything else to wear. Or how, when he'd told her that the pie she'd baked looked like it had been eaten before, she'd snatched it off the table and flung it out the kitchen door into the backyard.

I loved that. It sounded exciting. But they didn't seem to be doing it anymore. I never saw anyone fight, except children.

*Our* kind of people didn't seem to do that.

Being a member of high society wasn't the fun of going to Hamilton; the fun was doing so many of the things our mothers had done and told us about, and finding new things of our own.

I remember how, in the summer, we'd go out to "the place" to camp out on the Leon, and how Old Daddy would borrow a truck and have his town-bed put up on it, and we'd all drive down to where the pecan trees grew thick along the river bank, the wind blowing in our hair. Old Daddy had to have his comforts. He'd bring that bed down every summer, and a special rug that had to go beside it, and he had the blacksmith build him a little portable toilet so he could sit in comfort.

There was only a small cabin on the Leon River, so we kids slept outside and had a marvelous time. We'd swim and fish, and feed the sheep—one, called Old Whitey, would eat cottonseed cakes out of my hand—and raid the orchard for ripe peaches hot from the sun. We all loved to sing, and sometimes Old Daddy would play his banjo and we'd harmonize or accompany him with combs.

The town was small enough to be thoroughly explored, and we knew it all by heart by the time we were six. "Downtown" was located around the big old limestone courthouse surrounded by Bois d'Arc trees. In the fall, the school's Halloween carnival was held there. In the courthouse yard, along with the obligatory Confederate monument, there was a huge brass bell. When the Hamilton Bulldogs won a football game, everyone dashed for the courthouse—the first one there got to ring the bell. My mother, my uncle, and my aunt made that run all through their school years. I did, too, when I was older, and even won it once. In the summer, a haze of caliche dust hovered over all of it, caking our bare feet, sticking to even the leaves of the trees, whose heavy shade was only a little relief from the relentless Texas sun.

It was cool down in the square under the huge Bois d'Arc trees, but Mama didn't like for me to go there because the courthouse hangers-on used to sit on a rail all afternoon and tell stories and spit. The boys would go there with their B-B guns and shoot sparrows out of the trees, but Mama never let me go with them. "You're going to get shot," she'd say, "and get an eye put out." I got the idea very early that sports and rough games were not the kind of thing little girls did: little girls should look pretty and never get dirty. Getting dirty was for the boys, who seemed to have all the fun.

It didn't seem fair to me, but most of the other girls didn't seem to mind.

Mam-Ma and Old Daddy's house sat high up on one of the grassy hills that surrounded the town. The closest neighbors were the Blaylocks, who had two sons in high school and were always glad to see us—the boys turned over their tree house to us and the swing their daddy had put in the hundred-year-old oak tree in their side yard. The two houses were separated by a sea of Johnson grass that made a splendid jungle. The jungle came down eventually to make room for a house for Ben Blaylock's sister Eleanor and my Mam-Ma's brother, when they retired and moved to Hamilton. That made the hill a real family place.

Pam and I played on the front porch. In preparation for our visit, Mam-Ma would collect two large cardboard boxes from the hardware store, with his sharper-than-a-razor wee penknife, Old Daddy would cut windows and doors; and Pam and I would have a house apiece on opposite corners of the porch, where we would play Miz Lady, pay visits to each other, or sit and sulk when we got tired of each other's company.

As the years passed, more and more cousins joined us in Hamilton, Pam and I both got the brothers we had been promised and threatened with. "Hey, let's go over to the Littles' and play," somebody would suggest soon after we'd demolished a bushel of Mam-Ma's breakfast biscuits. We'd grab our air rifles and what we called nigger shooters—our sling shots—and try to make the getaway without the little brothers, Dick and Johnny. But there was no way.

When they were small they were a definite burden, because we played war at the Littles', just as our parents had when they were children. To the east of the Littles' house there was a vacant lot that had bunkers and trenches all over it—some of them older than the Maginot Line. In times of plenty and parental inattention, war was waged with air rifles. Otherwise, we made do with rocks and nigger shooters. I can still remember Charles Little chasing me all over that damned lot, with the sticks of his shooter poking me between the shoulder blades, yelling, "Surrender, you dirty Jap, surrender!"

The girls were always either the Germans or the Japanese or the Indians, depending on the movie that had played the Saturday before at the Strand Theater.

"No, no, I won't surrender," I gasped back at him. "Only, please please don't shoot!"

He shot, and I still have a scar on my back.

We played rough games, but it was rough country. The last lynching had taken place in my mother's girlhood; she remembered it well. There were no more Negroes in Hamilton County after that, and it was well known that none were welcome. Hamilton was almost as western as it was southern, and the last shoot-out occurred in the courthouse square in 1932, when the Gentry's Mill gang had it out with the local sheriff. There were still remnants of that family and several others my grandmother called "drag-nasties" or "the scrapings of the earth." Anybody else who didn't meet her social approval was simply "common."

Once, when John's father was running the weekly newspaper, he ran afoul of some of those folks my grandmother found so reprehensible. Evidently Dad had said something in the paper that didn't sit well, and he stepped out of his office late one evening and into a terrible fight. There were three of them, and before the melee was over, one had nearly gouged Dad's eye out.

Luckily Cousin Charlie was able to fix his eye, and most important, Dad had beat the living daylights out of all three of them, singlehandedly, and was a hero ever after.

Besides the newspaper work, John's father was also principal of the local high school and his mother taught history there. John's mother had been my Aunt Tink's favorite teacher, and was a good friend of my mother's. She used to love to tell me how when I was just a baby, on my first visit to Hamilton, she had gone for a drive with Mama and they had discussed at length whether boys or girls were easier to raise. John's mother was full of good advice for Mama; Little John was five years old and she knew the ropes. She used to laugh and say, "I never dreamed it was my daughter-in-law I was helping to raise!"

The war came, and Pappy went back to the Army and I became an ordinary Army brat. In eleven years of schooling, I went to eight different schools, in places as diverse as Japan and Arkansas, Manila and New Orleans. I learned that there was a lot more to the world than Hamilton, Texas, and a lot more kinds of people than I had found there. When Pappy was sent somewhere we couldn't go, we returned to Hamilton. It was always so good to be back where everybody knew who I was, where nothing had to be *explained*.

Everybody knew everything.

As I got older, that became a nuisance instead of a comfort. I never had a date without the neighbors' commenting on who he was, where we went, what we did there, and the time we got back home. My friends, my behavior, my dress—everything—was subject to the most constant scrutiny. And critical comment. And comparison with my mother, "who at your age . . ."

"Mama, why does everybody have to be so damned nosy? Why can't they just mind their own stupid business and *leave me alone?*"

"Please don't say ugly words, baby," Mama corrected absently. "It's not that they're so nosy—it's just that they love you, and care about what you do."

Later, when I was a freshman in high school, I dated an older boy who used to take me home early and then go see a girl we all knew was "common." I'd stand at my window and watch his car go down the hill as far as her house, enraged at the unfairness of it all. But there were "good"

girls and "bad" girls, and one's reputation had to be preserved at all costs. Mama lectured me regularly on it, and
so did all the other mothers I knew, for all my friends
were strictly behaved.

I gave my watchers precious little to be shocked about—
when I was young and when I was in high school. Com-
pared to some of my friends, in the Camp Fire Girls Circle that John's mother sponsored, I wasn't even that much
of a tomboy. I made good grades in school, I kept my
clothes neat and clean, and I had good manners. I was everything a sweet little girl, my mama's sweet little girl,
was supposed to be. Most of the time. But there were
times when the confinement got to be just too much to
bear; times when I'd decide to run away and play with the
boys.

They were never too glad to see me.

"Get out of here, you crummy, chicken-dopey-crybaby
GIRL!"

I hung around the Tarzan place on the creek in their ab-
sence, early in the morning and after supper, until I got
up the courage to try the swing. It was a rope contraption,
with burlap sacks for a seat. It was a perilous climb up the
tree to the branch on which it was attached, then came the
breath-taking drop as you swung out over the creek, and
then you let go—I was the only girl who'd do it. When I
confronted the boys with my accomplishment, and de-
manded to be allowed to join the Tarzan game, there was
a long, whispered conference.

How could I play, I was a girl. "Jane!" somebody suggested. There was a chorus of retching sounds—who
needed *Jane?* Finally, a compromise was struck.

I got to be Cheetah.

There were other things that girls were allowed to do. It

was okay for girls to ride horses, and a few of us went at that with wild abandon. I was lucky—my Uncle Edben who lived in nearby Dublin was a big shot on the rodeo committee. The rodeo was the one and only Grand National Championship Rodeo, and the first performance was held in Dublin every year before it moved to Madison Square Garden. When we were very small, we got to ride in the parades in a stagecoach. As we grew bigger, we rode our own horses in the parade and the Grand Entry, and finally graduated to working as wranglers—bringing the horses into town for the dignitaries to ride, collecting them, and caring for them after every performance.

Listening to the rodeo performers talk about New York gave that place an immediacy for me. I brought their stories about the tall buildings, the adventure, the excitement, back to my friend Maryann in Hamilton. Maryann wasn't all that satisfied with our small world either; she wanted to be an actress. We'd sit in the farthest corner of her backyard, trying to escape the relentless piano scales played by her mother's pupils; we smoked cedar bark, and speculated about our future in the big city. Maryann was adamant.

"I have five hundred dollars in the bank now; my grandmother gives me fifty dollars every Christmas. As soon as I'm old enough, I'll have enough money to go." Sure enough, at the end of her sophomore year at TCU, she wrote her parents a short note, withdrew her savings, and came to New York. And, after years of very hard work, she did become an actress.

It took me a whole lot longer to get there.

For one thing, I wasn't sure exactly what I wanted to be. Perhaps a painter, or a dress designer, or maybe a writer. I just wanted to be somebody, somebody important. I didn't know how to go about that.

There weren't that many ways to be important in Hamilton. You could be important if you were a football player. John B. Sullivan, Jr., was important then, and I remember him in his red and black Bulldogs letter jacket. He was ages older—a full five years—and already a high-school football hero when he'd appear at our Camp Fire Girls meetings to carry in the cases of soda pop. He remembers nothing but a passel of giggly little girls, but I can remember all of us oh-my-ing and being very impressed. One story I remember from those days was about how John, who played center, had once picked up a fumble and run for a touchdown—all the while his father, who had run college track, peddled backward along the sidelines, keeping up with him, cheering him on.

Well, I couldn't be a football player.

My great-grandfather Perry, Old Granddad, was important, too; he was president of the bank and lived in one of the biggest houses in town. When we went to the picture show in town on Saturday, my cousins and I would always stop by first to pay him a visit. We would wait politely outside the fence around his desk while he came to "a stopping place"; then he would take us all into the vault, past all the safety-deposit boxes, beyond the big, round door with all the dials and locks and alarms. In the nether reaches of the vault, he'd produce the largest bill he had on hand, and let each of us hold it for a second or two. Then he'd present each of us with a brand-new, never-used-before, one-dollar bill of our very own. I thought he must be very rich.

Old Granddad was something of a hero, too. He'd

never been in any fights that I knew about, never gotten his eye gouged out or played football, but he was a very important man all the same. His was the only bank for miles and miles around that didn't fail during the Depression. Out of his own pocket he had saved farms all over the county from foreclosure. Most people in town regarded him with love and great respect.

There were only heroes in Hamilton, no heroines. Instead, in my family and outside it, the remarkable women were the eccentrics—their peculiarities ranging from a mild disregard for convention to genuine dottiness.

If you were a woman you really couldn't be independent, and socially acceptable, until you reached some magic age. For the most part, they were older women who just didn't fit into the mold—who would really want to be like them? But for as long as I can remember I was attracted to these women.

They did what they goddamn well pleased, and I admired them for it.

One of my favorites was a dear friend of my mother's who lived with her lawyer-husband in a lovely Cape Cod house across town from my grandmother. Thaddeus and Louise had never had any children of their own and welcomed us all to their house and yard. John remembers being allowed to roller skate in their attic on rainy days; I went there to listen to Louise's Debussy records and cry, and look at her art books. I fell in love with Botticelli there when I was nine years old.

My own family had its share of wonderful, zany women. My great-grandmother, who built her own furniture for a hobby, didn't give a rap for what anyone thought of her. Miss Molly dipped snuff, and when I once asked her if I could have a taste, she let me try it. It was loathsome. So I asked her, "Oh, Granny, how can you *stand* this awful stuff?"

"I don't like it very much," she said. "I just took to dipping because it made Mr. Perry so mad."

Something certainly must have, for she and Mr. Perry had gotten a divorce nearly forty years before. I never knew exactly why. Divorce was still frowned upon in Hamilton, so at the turn of the century it must have caused a real scandal. If so, it didn't daunt Miss Molly. She built her furniture and puttered in her garden just as before.

After her divorce from Old Granddad, a sister from West Texas, three hundred miles away, wrote to her asking if she remembered a certain bachelor, who wanted to marry her now that she was free. Miss Molly did. So she made all the arrangements, packed, closed up her house, got in the wagon, and drove off.

She got as far as Priddy, a little, teeny town about twenty miles west of Hamilton, and remembered a gentleman who lived there. She decided to hell with it, she wasn't going to make that long trip to West Texas when there was a nice, eligible man so handy. So she married Papa Billy, from Priddy.

Meanwhile, Old Granddad began seeing Miss Ida, whom everyone referred to as "that hat trimmer from St. Louis." Legend has it Old Granddad came to call on her one day and Miss Ida pulled a gun on him and said: "Mr. Perry, you're going to marry me."

And he did.

I never knew if the story was true or not. Miss Ida died of the flu long before I was born, and no one in the family could confirm it. But I loved the story just the same; it made me giggle every time I saw my reserved and dignified great-grandfather, who was so formidable that all his wives called him "Mr. Perry."

When Miss Ida died, he married Miss Amanda, who was also somewhat eccentric. For one thing, she insisted on doing everything for herself. Everything. John, who lived across the street from her, remembers being sent to Miss Amanda's to borrow some milk. She didn't answer his knock at first, but then he heard her yoo-hooing from the backyard, and when he went around back he found her wearing a pince-nez and a fur coat, milking the cow.

My Aunt Eleanor had wanted to be a concert pianist but married my uncle instead. When they built their house on the hill, in what had been the Johnson grass jungle, a platform was built in the living room for Aunt Eleanor's grand piano. She often played it for me, telling me to lie down underneath it, on the platform, and to close my eyes, the better to hear the music.

It has taken me so many years to hear Hamilton music again. I loved the place because it was home to me, even though I never felt at home there after I was eleven or twelve.

There had to come a time when the soft golden haze that ringed the limestone courthouse on the square in summer just turned into the powdery caliche dust it really was.

There came a time when the Bois d'Arc and oak trees weren't the most beautiful trees I'd ever seen, and the rolling hills of Graves pasture looked pretty tacky to my eyes. I wanted too much to be other places—bigger and more exciting places. I didn't understand that Hamilton was such a special place—old-fashioned, small, self-satisfied, and self-contained.

# 2

## Uprootings

Neither the southern tradition of Hamilton nor the Army tradition that was always so much of my life take very kindly to rebellion. When Pappy was in Virginia Military Institute, he once rode a steeplechase on a rebellious horse that refused one of the jumps; when the horse stopped, sharply, Pappy was catapulted over the jump himself. He got up calmly, brushed some of the dirt off, walked around the barricade, took the reins, gave the horse a long look, then socked him right between the eyes, knocking him colder than a mackerel.

What amazes and astounds me now, as I sift through all these memories, is that *my* rebellion—leaving John and Kathleen, the most rebellious act I'd ever heard of—came from someone with such a deep and solid grounding in those dual traditions. Couple this with the fact that in so many ways I had a *happy* childhood. I wanted for nothing; I loved and respected my parents and they loved me. Looking back now, I cannot see that I was really any different from any of the other little girls who were my friends in Hamilton. We all had dotty older female relations, we all chafed at the restrictions from time to time, we all got into some mischief. My early years were happy and contented, in an environment that was loving and in every way secure. What reason did I have to rebel?

But if my childhood was "settled," my years of adolescence were certainly not. They were restless, impermanent times, in which great expectations often led to nagging disappointments; the changes were usually dramatic. Up until then, everything had happened as it was supposed to; perhaps, if the tranquil times had continued, I would have turned out the way *I* was supposed to.

But suddenly the war broke out. Pappy was immediately assigned to Fort Hood, in Waco, Texas, and during the next ten years we also lived in Colorado Springs; New Orleans; Macon, Georgia; Manila, P.I.; Jacksonville, Arkansas; Japan; and San Antonio. My life went through a series of uprootings—all upsetting, frustrating—and all accompanied by a few more than the normal upheavals of adolescence.

I had to learn to shift for myself, adapt to new houses, new schools, new friends; and always, I was "the new girl." By the time I was seventeen, I was still conventional enough to want only the things other girls my age did—to be popular, to be pretty, to be a cheerleader—but just enough restlessness and questioning had taken root to make me want other things as well. I found to my amazement that I could be willful and rebellious enough to do something that wounded my mother deeply.

I became like Pappy's horse which refused the jump.

Less than a year after the peace treaty was signed with Japan, we joined Pappy in the Philippines, where he was in command of a division of Filipino scouts, still rousting the Japanese out of the hills.

Wars are never suddenly over, and this one surely wasn't. During the short time we lived in the military compound in Manila, the guards would get nervous patroling at night and begin to shoot at each other.

"Hit the dirt!" our two Filipino housemaids would shout in a fright, and we did, hugging the floor while the bullets made a sieve out of the corrugated tin roof.

After a month we moved to Camp O'Donnell, which had been the final destination of the death march from Bataan; it had been a prison camp. There was no school and no commissary. We sometimes had to make do with C-rations; when supplies got through, canned asparagus might be our only vegetable for a month, can after can of it. I'd been a picky eater until then; I soon learned to eat anything that didn't eat me first or crawl off the plate.

With no school, no milk, and tropical diseases galore, snakes, bugs, and people still shooting at each other and sometimes us—the Islands were a nightmare for my mother. To me and my brother Dick it was a beautiful, exciting place, full of forests and jungles, half the world's birds, monkeys, and water buffalo. When we weren't busy playing Terry and the Pirates with the three other "unfortunate" Army brats next door, I was reading my way through the camp's library—especially every lurid historical novel I could find.

Mama's anxieties were not helped any by the Division's doctor. A pediatrician in civilian life, he must have been frustrated by having only five children to fuss over, for he came to see us every day, feeding us prodigious amounts of atrabine to ward off malaria, lamenting the inadequacies of our diet, and expressing amazement that we all managed to stay so healthy.

He should have paid more attention to Mama, for it was she who got sick—with malaria and dysentery all at once. She had to be taken back to Manila to the hospital, and almost died there. She eventually came home to us, still very weak, and as soon as she was well enough to travel we all returned to the States.

I should have been happy to be returning to Hamilton, but that was not a happy time. On the ship coming home, my world really fell apart. My parents broke the news that they had decided to get a divorce. Mama, Dick, and I would be going back to Hamilton without Pappy.

My parents had never exchanged so much as a cross word in front of us. They had always been polite; I had always thought, without thinking, they would always love each other. And now they were saying they couldn't be married anymore, couldn't get along. I couldn't believe it. *What on earth could be wrong?*

"It's going to be all right," Mama tried to assure me. "No matter what happens your Pappy and I will always love you." Couldn't anything be counted on to last? Marriage was supposed to be forever. "Soon we'll be back at home with Mam-Ma and Old Daddy, and everything will be just fine."

But it wasn't just fine, not this time.

All my old friends laughed at me—the atrabine had turned my skin, even the whites of my eyes, a bright yellow. And we were so thin, all three of us, my Mam-Ma cried when she saw us. When I told my "war stories," the ones my daughter Kathleen later loved to hear when she was little, my friends told me I was the biggest liar who ever lived. My yarns about the straw house on stilts, the

twelve-foot-long snake I'd seen my father blast to smither-
eens with his .45, the Moro headhunters we'd met while
looking for a Christmas tree, the earthquakes and vol-
canoes, and best of all, *no school*—all that was just too
much for any Hamilton fourth-grader to swallow.

I spent much of that time by myself—up in the tree
house or reading my way through the local library. Miss
Matty Oliver, the librarian, kept a weather eye on my
book consumption and weaned me away from trash with
Pearl Buck and *Anthony Adverse*. We went on to Dumas,
Dickens, and Tolstoy. *Winesburg, Ohio* I discovered on my
own.

Miss Matty couldn't help when it came to the problem of
my parents. I brooded a lot about that, up in the tree
house by myself.

I couldn't understand what had happened between
them; each of them still had only kind things to say of the
other. I tried being mad at my father; after all, he had left
us alone for so long.

"But it isn't your Pappy's fault," Mama insisted.

I began to think that perhaps it was mine. Maybe it was
because my brother and I fought so much. So I tried very
hard not to fight. I tried to please in everything, and do
what was expected of me.

One thing expected of me always, throughout my whole
childhood, was to look pretty. My head-to-foot yellows
didn't help—and to make matters worse, suddenly I became, as children often do at that age, very myopic. I
remember waiting in the outer office one day while Mama
conferred with the doctor. When she came out, I could see
she'd been crying. I'd have to wear glasses for the rest of
my life he had told her—at least when I wanted to see
anything. Without them I was blind as a toad.

Both my parents waited a year, with their typical propriety, and then both remarried. Each marriage was a shock to me: I was not told about either of them until afterwards.

My mother married another Army officer, one who had served with my father several years before. He was a quiet man, gentler and less career-obsessed than Pappy. He lived only to make my mother happy, and certainly he did just that for the rest of her life. My brother Dick and I went to live with him and Mama, and he was unfailingly good to us, if at times somewhat distant. He left our guidance and discipline to Mama, but by example taught me some powerful lessons. Papa Pete was the most self-disciplined man I have ever known—he once taught himself shorthand because he thought it might be useful. He was a great admirer of Francis Bacon and quoted him with frustrating frequency—but just as *observations*, never as advice.

Discipline. It was something I'd have to learn. Someday.

Milly, my stepmother, frightened me at first. I'd never known a woman as tough and independent before. Pappy had known her in the Philippines, where she'd been with the Red Cross. She'd seen more combat, and in both the European and Pacific theaters, than he. From a large Virginia family, Milly had put herself through college on swimming and diving scholarships. I could not imagine such a thing—a woman athlete!

Dick and I began spending our summers in Fort Worth with them, and the first thing she tried to do was to make a swimmer out of me. I wasn't too interested; I could swim well enough to keep from drowning, and besides, it cut heavily into my reading time. But Milly was insistent.

Standing on the edge of the pool, toes gripping the tile, knowing the water was going to be colder than blue floozians, I'd hesitate. Without ceremony, Milly's strong foot would be not-so-gently brought into conjunction with the seat of my tank suit, and in I'd go. As soon as I surfaced, sputtering for air, there she'd be in the water beside me, laughing and shouting: "Swim, damnit, swim! If I had your long legs, I'd have been an Olympic champion!"

I tried, out of a manic desire to please, but my heart was never in it. I already had the conviction that a young girl's body—and her mind as well—were mysteriously fragile.

In a small town in the South, a girl's chief preparation for high school was dancing lessons and carefully supervised dancing parties. The boys, who had been our tormentors for so long, had to learn to get along on our turf now. They came to the parties the mothers gave, reluctant and reeking of Old Spice—but they came.

I still had the same friends I'd had as a child—the daughters of my mother's friends. We all, somehow, learned the complex and elaborate rituals and postures of young southern ladies. We learned the "southern radar." I still don't know precisely how it's taught, but "good" southern girls learn it fast and early. It is part of the politics of survival. You learn to live by your intuition, to know what others—particularly men—are feeling, and what they expect from you. You learn to please—before a request is even made—and to sense an emotional climate and how to manipulate it. If someone displeases or hurts you, you make sure he *knows* it. It's done without words, without loud argument, but the message is clear: *Yes, I'm hurt. You've hurt me. It's your fault I'm so hurt.*

I suppose I did it to John in later years, along with the self-sacrifice *for* him and *to* myself—for sacrifice was something I learned too. And filial duty. And how to protect appearances. And much, much more.

At slumber parties, as teen-agers, we girls would practice the less subtle art of becoming *femmes fatales* together. We practiced fixing each other's hair, tried out facial expressions and make-up in front of the mirror, dressed up in each other's clothes. We gossiped incessantly about the "older men"—boys in the senior class, boys on the football team.

The only hope for ever attracting the attention of these lofty beings was to be utterly gorgeous. So we thought. But even that didn't always work. Maryann, the aspiring actress, actually was—and they paid as little attention to her as they did to the rest of us. Still, that was supposed to be the magic key. At least once a day I'd stare into the big pier-glass mirror in my grandmother's front bedroom and catalog my faults and shortcomings: my hair, too straight; my eyes, too small and too close together (and strictly ornamental at that); my nose, too short; mouth, too big; bosom, too flat; waist, too big; legs, too spindly; feet, too small to go with any of it.

Whatever my personal flaws, Hamilton was still home. I was accepted—even popular—and I was anxiously looking forward to being elected cheerleader . . . when we got our orders for Japan.

Another change.

The Korean war had cooled down enough for dependent travel to begin again, so Papa Pete had sent for us. In Kyoto, our big Japanese house—walled and gardened— was perfect for the parties Mama loved to give and gave so well. And the old capital city itself was beautiful and gracious. But the high school was a jolt.

After Hamilton, it was like being on another planet. My classmates smoked and drank; many of them did other forbidden things as well. I was torn between my old ways and this fast new world I'd suddenly been thrown into.

Mama was troubled by the tension she soon saw in me and disturbed even more by some of my new friends. She had no use at all for Tony, my boyfriend, who was Italian, Catholic, and the son of an immigrant sergeant. "You'll see, baby," she warned. "They're just not our kind of people."

They certainly weren't.

The family was big and boisterous, Tony's mama and papa spoke Italian most of the time, and often with a lot of decibels. I liked them all enormously. When Tony dropped out of school, joined the Army, and was shipped back to the States, I thought my heart would break. I also thought my mother was an awful snob and told her so. My age plus the independence this gypsy life had forced on me made some of Mama's ideas and injunctions a bit hard to take.

My resistance didn't sway her, and she remained especially firm on one point: people from divergent backgrounds were incompatible. Even in Kyoto, she still preserved the continuity and values she'd lived with all her life. Most of it no longer made sense to me. Wandering through the city on weekends, exploring the temples, the parks of this different culture, meeting people like Tony from different backgrounds, my views were becoming confused. *My mother is so small-town,* I thought. *I love her so dearly but I just don't see things the way she does anymore.*

But another part of me held onto those same things—encouraging me to do what I was supposed to do. In my second year in Japan, I began dating the son of a surgeon, and together we won every major office and honor in the school. Whatever he was president of, I was vice-president of—and vice-versa; he was captain of the basketball team and I was head cheerleader. I loved the limelight. We were convinced the principal couldn't make any kind of decision regarding the school without our advice and consent, he called us into his office so frequently for *ex-officio* conferences. We were superkids—clean-cut, bright, and all-American.

I was happy in Kyoto. My life was full, every moment busy, and I couldn't wait to begin my senior year.

Then Papa Pete was ordered to return to the States.

This move was back to Texas, but to San Antonio this time. And San Antonio proved to be a nightmare.

Although we rented a house on the south side of town, Dick and I were sent to school on the far north side. The Sullivans had moved to San Antonio a few years before and John's father was the principal there. Mama said she'd just feel better if her old friend could keep an eye on us.

All the kids at Edison High had known each other since Noah was a rag doll; it was a society as closed as Hamilton's, only this time I had no credentials. Football was the be-all and end-all, and if you weren't a player, or one of the cheerleaders—who'd all been picked the year before I got there—you simply *weren't*. As a new senior, the only newcomer in a class of one hundred fifty, I wasn't even a curiosity. Just a freak. The girls were nice to me at school but seldom invited me to their parties. The boys classified me as a "brain" and a "wierd-o." No one in that school asked me for a date all year. I couldn't believe it. Nothing like it had ever happened to me before. I buried myself in school work.

Mama was even more worried than I was about my absolute lack of social success. "You're not *very* smart, you know," she teased—but the message was pretty clear: "If you were *really* smart, you'd learn to play a little dumb. Boys don't like girls who are smarter than they are!"

Pappy was blunter. "Too bad your brother got all the looks and you got all the brains."

To compound my miseries, when my seventeenth birthday came that fall, I had to face the shattering fact that I was always going to be flat chested. I'd been told, and I believed it, that I'd soon "fill out"; but Mama's curves, which I'd always counted on inheriting, had somehow missed me in the gene sort.

I enlisted the aid of a Hidden Treasure bra. A long series of them. A treacherous garment, it had a way of acquiring dents; the wearer had to be ever watchful. Books had to be carried in one's hand, never up against the chest. For dancing and other contact sports, it was safest to use a little padding. Gym socks did nicely.

But gym socks were a poor substitute for the real thing. I felt outraged and cheated. If nature had made me a girl, why couldn't nature make me look more like one? I smiled a great deal, hoping that might compensate; I had pretty teeth. Mama suggested I gain weight. But the fifteen pounds I gained by diligently attacking her good cooking and milkshakes somehow never made their way to my bosom. Once thin and shapeless, I merely became fat and shapeless through heavy eating. I introduced myself to the miseries of dieting.

Finally, I met a very bookish boy from another high

school. James was a member of the Texas Pioneers, a young peoples' social club that went in heavily for tea dances and cotillions. Letters were sent from Hamilton, establishing my pedigree, and I, too, became a Texas Pioneer.

I soon realized why Mama was so relieved that my social life had survived the crisis. She had quietly been planning, for who knows how many years, that I make a debut in Abilene. She must have gone to some of the balls in Abilene when we lived there; she may even have envied the debutantes—and hoped, all those years, that she herself could someday experience that excitement *through* me. I soon found out that she'd worked tenaciously at it—keeping up with all the right people, some of whom she hadn't seen in years; writing letters and pulling strings. She was absolutely determined that I should have that debut.

At first I wouldn't even listen to her.

But I could see, as her elaborate preparations continued, how important it was to her. And I was perfectly miserable at the thought of disappointing her.

All I knew about debuts and debutantes came from pictures in the newspapers, from books and *Vogue* magazine. Nobody I knew in San Antonio was coming out. I didn't even like the expression.

"Oh, baby, there are parties beforehand—tea dances and luncheons . . ."

"But I don't know any of those people," I protested.

"Of course you do. They used to come to your birthday parties when you were little."

"Well," I said tentatively, "what would I have to do?"

She brightened. "Well, after the parties, there's the ball

itself. You'd wear a long, white dress and long, white gloves—you can even wear my good kid gloves if you promise to be careful."

I couldn't see any sense in it all.

"The country club ballroom is all decorated for Christmas," Mama continued, sensing a lessening in my resistance, "and they have a special thing all fixed up at one end of the room—it looks like Cinderella's coach. As each Christmas Belle is introduced she steps through the coach . . ."

"Oh, no, Mama!"

"She steps through the coach with her escort and makes her bow."

Cinderella's coach! Somebody had to be crazy! I wasn't about to go all the way to Abilene just to make a fool of myself trying to be a phony Cinderella. A debut seemed nothing less than a humongous waste of money, energy, and time.

I knew how it appealed to Mama. I knew how much it meant to her.

I made my first independent stand. I would not do it. I don't know where my resistance came from—from intuition perhaps, or perhaps a slowly dawning realization that I could not—would not—live that kind of life. But instead of taking pride in that realization, I found that arguing with Mama, standing up for something that involved *my* life, made me feel perfectly dreadful. I didn't want to disappoint her. I knew she wanted with all her heart for me to have that debut.

We were still deep in discussion when something happened that took the matter out of our hands. One afternoon at school, showing off the cheerleader gymnastics

I'd learned in Japan, I came too slowly out of a backflip. I landed smack on my face, and skidded five feet on the asphalt. My face looked like hamburger meat.

I was rushed to Brook Army Medical Center, where one of the Army's best plastic surgeons spent hours reconstructing my upper lip, scrubbing the asphalt out of the rest of my face, and telling me that everything was going to be perfectly fine.

In the movies, when you have plastic surgery, they swathe your head in bandages—I didn't even have a Band-Aid—and unveil you as Elizabeth Taylor. I was left with my face terribly bruised, my upper lip swollen like a poisoned pup, and one huge scab from hairline to chin. James came to see me, and winced. Mama nearly cried her eyes out.

I was devastated. I'd never thought I was especially pretty before—now everybody was telling me how pretty I *used* to be. If, as I'd been taught, my face was supposed to be my fortune, I was now almost certainly bankrupt.

Though the scars healed rapidly, just as the doctor promised, the rest of me didn't. I didn't want to go to school. I didn't want to have anything to do with the new clothes my mother bought me while I was in the hospital. I didn't want to do anything but be left alone. If I could just get away from San Antonio, my life might be manageable. I looked forward to going off to college, to doing some serious work. *I'll be away from all this, forever.*

Then all of Mama's elaborate planning bore fruit.

The debut invitation, which she had longed for for so many months, which she had planned for for so many years, finally arrived. In December, it said, I could become one of Abilene Country Club's twelve Christmas Belles.

Mama was ecstatic. I could see the joy and triumph on her face as she rushed to show me the invitation.

I looked at it carefully. I could imagine the *me* I always saw in the mirror, the me that never looked quite right, all gussied up in a white ballgown, clambering out of a papier mâché coach in front of a bunch of strangers, all of whom were watching, waiting for me to fall on my face.

"I can't do it," I told Mama quietly.

"Baby, please. It will be so good for you, so important . . ."

I felt awful. I wasn't a willing rebel; I had almost never rebelled before. I wanted, with all my heart, to do the right thing, as I'd always tried to do what was expected of me. And I knew how hard she'd worked for this. I felt anxious, nervous, queasy when I said, "I don't want to do it, Mama." Even a fairy godmother couldn't have talked me into it. Mama couldn't.

When I told her it would cost too much, she said, "We'll manage."

"I'd rather have the money for college. I *need* that—I don't need a debut, Mama."

"*Please?*"

I looked at the invitation in my hands and, without saying a word, tore it up.

# 3

## In Tune
## With the Universe

Spring came to San Antonio, and so did John B. Sullivan, Jr., home on leave from Fort Ord in California.

One day his father summoned me to his office over the school intercom. He'd done it before, and I'd bring him the piece of homemade pie Mama always put in my lunch, and we'd tell each other stories and visit. Like everybody else who ever knew him well, I adored "Big John."

This time, when I walked into the office, he wasn't alone. "You remember Little John, don't you, Judy? Little 'un, this is Miss Fairy Foot." He smiled, relieved me of the piece of pecan pie, and left the office, shutting the door behind him.

Little John wasn't so little any more—not that he ever had been as far as I could remember. But now he was certainly all grown up, and quite handsome, with rugged features, curly black hair, and Irish green eyes.

I made myself comfortable in his father's office and we began talking about Hamilton and the people we'd both known. Soon a class bell rang, and I reluctantly excused myself and headed for the door, only to discover it had been locked from the other side.

Big John was up to his tricks again.

So we settled in, had a nice long visit, and I told John about my plans for college and my ambition to become as good a teacher as his mother was. After a little more than an hour, our jailer reappeared, full of chuckles and very fishy-sounding apologies for having locked the door "by mistake."

John offered to drive me home.

"Oh, it's awfully far," I protested, hoping he didn't know how far it really was.

He assured me that didn't matter; he had to take his eleven-year-old sister Ellen to her piano lesson anyway.

Ellen never made it to her piano lesson. We drove to my house, and she happily played football with Dick while John and I got better acquainted on the porch.

We had a date that night, and every night thereafter until he had to return to California. We spent most of them talking—about his plans, and mine. John had finished his BA degree in English and history, and had already taught a year in one of the San Antonio high schools. His parents were an inspiration for both of us. John was anxious to get out of the service and return to graduate school and to teaching. He was as much fun as his daddy, as sweet as his mama, and smart like both of them. I was so taken with him I couldn't see straight.

Mama, ever watchful of my social life, was delighted; I was ecstatic. When news that we were dating made its way to Hamilton, there was a flurry of excitement from the relatives and friends of both families. Everyone approved.

That was nice, but there was still the matter of college.

Instead of talking with other people about it, I should have spent more time consulting my parents. As it turned out, they didn't seem to be attaching quite the same importance to it that I was.

Pappy had talked for years about my going to Sweetbriar, where his sister had gone. I felt the same way about a finishing school as I did about the debut—I wanted no part of it. I knew I'd never fit in at Sweetbriar, and I certainly didn't want to get "finished"; I hadn't even gotten started yet.

There was a great vagueness surrounding the whole business. When I expressed no desire to go to Sweetbriar, Pappy's interest faded. Money was very tight, it seemed. I pursued the matter. Yes, I learned some money had been put aside for Dick, who had never been a very good student. But he was the male child and would have to support a family someday. He must have an education. I could hardly believe it. *No one had made any real provision for me to go to school.*

"We'll manage *something*," Mama promised. She must have known what I was feeling. Mama had never gone to college, had not been able to go because of the Depression. Again money had been tight, so only one child could be sent—her brother Edben. She had always been sorry she'd missed out on the fun. She didn't want me to.

In the end, Mama scrimped and juggled her budget, and essentially sent me to school out of her household money.

The distinction between good and mediocre colleges was mercifully unknown to me—it would have only added another frustration. In Texas in those days, a college's chief claim to excellence and prestige was its football team.

The school I chose in the end didn't even have a football

team. But it was supercheap. Room and board at Texas State College for Women was less expensive than at any of the other Texas schools, and the college provided all textbooks. As for my offer to live in a co-op, where I'd help cook meals and share housekeeping chores, or to try to find a part-time job, Mama wouldn't hear of it. These weren't the kind of things she wanted me to be doing.

I began with high hopes and expectations that now that I was finally in college, school would be exciting and a challenge. But there wasn't much to love in "Tessie." It was dreary, provincial, and while the art classes I had so looked forward to were better than the rest, good grades depended more on simple elbow grease than brains.

But my two art teachers were marvelous.

Unmarried eccentrics, they had the delightful names of Lucinda Swann and Oriane Charbonneaux. Miss Swann, though older than my mother, seemed so much younger, with her intense interest in her work, in art. She was proper and reserved, very British, and she lived alone in a small, exquisitely decorated house. Now and then she'd sell some work and immediately do something rash—like buy a silver tea service. She would bring it to class so we could share its beauty. "Lovely, isn't it?" she'd say. "And to think I could have wasted all that money paying off some of my debts!" She was kind to me, and took a close interest in my work.

Miss Charbonneaux, a wild—and wildly different—woman lived in an apartment which looked as if it never had been furnished: somebody had accidentally left a few old, unmatched chairs and tables here and there. Books, papers, drawings, canvases were strewn all over. She didn't notice. Sometimes I wondered if she even noticed where she was; there were a few times when she stormed into class and lectured the whole hour in French or Italian.

In the beginning I had a few more dates than most of the girls I knew—which meant anything over the one-a-week ration for freshmen—thanks to friends from Hamilton who were at North Texas, the co-ed university across town. Mama became mildly concerned about my sex life, because I had rashly written that some of my friends actually *petted* on dates. I wrote because I was so flattened by it—terrified, too. More frightening, I knew that some of my friends had "gone all the way"—something so utterly foolhardy, to my way of thinking, I could never have told my mother, afraid it would give her a sick headache for a week.

The warnings I'd been getting since I was sixteen intensified. They came weekly by mail and verbally on holidays, reminders that boys often couldn't control their "feelings," and always ending with the admonition: "You know, baby, you simply *must* protect your reputation. A boy will not respect you if you let him go too far, and nice boys always want to marry nice girls."

Those strong feelings filled the mild Texas night air like ozone, heavy and full of menace. About all they meant to me was the danger of getting pregnant. I used to have nightmare fantasies about having to tell my parents I was pregnant, being expelled from school—which was the punishment in those days—either having to marry some guy who was too strong or too smart to be stopped in time, or having to hide out in a Florence Crittenton Home and give up the baby for adoption.

But what about *my* strong feelings?

They never had a chance, for I kept them wrapped up tightly in my crossed arms and legs. My stepmother

Milly, whose advice was more lighthearted than my mother's, told me: "Have a good time, just don't let them get into your pants." I couldn't see how she could dismiss the problem so flippantly. I listened to Mama instead. She seemed to have a better grasp of the gravity of the situation.

After a third no-score date, boys quit calling. Instead, they called on girls who weren't "stingy," "frigid," "teasers," or "lezzies." What else could explain why I wouldn't give in after being so persuasively courted with movies, hamburgers, and a good deal of pawing and heavy breathing?

Luckily, my emotions were engaged elsewhere. John wrote from California and then Korea with increasing frequency and seriousness. Every three days, three at a time, came his long, sweet, hilariously funny letters. They brought the kind of support and encouragement and approval I desperately needed. He could be strong-willed and strong-minded; I was especially impressed with the idealism with which he wrote about teaching.

When he came home that spring, I don't think he ever formally proposed to me, but soon we found ourselves talking about getting married.

Marriage.

I had never thought about *not* marrying. Sooner or later I knew it was the thing I must do. After my chaotic adolescence, my disappointment with Tessie, and the powerful feelings I was having, *sooner* seemed to make a lot of sense.

I was eighteen and very immature, but the idea was powerfully appealing. Marriage, that spring, meant freedom—from restrictive dormitory rules and accountability to my parents. John was planning to take his master's and to teach history in San Antonio; marrying him, I thought, meant I'd be able to do as I pleased.

Of course marriage had to do with love, too. Married was what you got when you fell in love, and John and I were sure to be best friends and constant lovers, *forever*.

I loved John very much. Married, we could have sex; I'd thought it would be nice to have it anyway, one way or the other, but he was adamant that we wait until after the wedding, and so wait we did.

John's parents were so much in favor of the match there were jokes about it being arranged. Mama felt I was too young, but she thought John a good choice; if married people had to have common backgrounds, we qualified admirably. We had our Hamilton roots in common, and we shared at that time a similar set of values—we even liked the same kinds of food. Of course I hadn't learned to cook any of it, nor had I learned to keep house; Mama had always taken care of a house beautifully, seemingly without expending much energy or interest.

What could there be to it?

"It's easy enough," she told me. "Anyone can do it, and it's something you'll have to do yourself only until you can afford to have a woman do it for you." It was clearly my responsibility, woman's work—but I didn't give it a moment's thought.

I felt I was too young, too, but I figured I'd never do any better than John, no matter how long I waited. I admired and loved him deeply, and it would be a good marriage—I *knew* it would. John was extremely handsome, full of exciting plans for his future. He was bright, witty, and articulate, he listened to me and took me seriously. I was impressed with him myself, delighted and amazed in fact that he would be so taken with me. My friends, whose opinions I valued far above my own, were also impressed; they liked and respected him. Their approval and ratification was important to me.

I knew that John had rather gotten himself into a marrying frame of mind. He wanted to get married soon, and if I didn't marry him right away, somebody else surely would. There were several very pretty girls waiting in the wings.

John would be a good person to be married to. What appealed to me most about him was his self-confidence, probably because I had so little of it myself. He'd take care of me far better than my parents had done. He'd shelter and protect me, bring order and stability back into my life, take up for me in arguments, keep me from being lonesome at night. I was ready to give my life over to him—go wherever he wanted or needed to go, do whatever he required of me, have his children and raise them, make a home for all of us.

Whatever stirrings of ambitions I had had in the past— to paint or to write—were subsumed to that. I could do them on the side.

"I just don't see what you see in him," said Miss Charbonneaux, one of the few dissenters. Miss Swann also disapproved, but what did they know? I didn't want to end up like them some day—living alone, scraping every nickel together for a brief trip somewhere to study or paint during the summer. I hadn't been prepared for such a life. The truth is, I pitied them. "He's nice but rather ordinary," Miss Charbonneaux said. "And he'll waste your life and energy and talent."

I didn't think so.

So it was settled.

Almost immediately the vast machinery—elaborate as Texas politics and quite unstoppable—was put into motion. We would be married July 1st, in Hamilton, and there would be an enormous party at the Perry Country Club.

Everybody was wondrously happy about the wedding. For the first time in my life, I was doing something I was *supposed* to do and liking it. I felt marvelously in tune with the universe.

# 4

## A Great
## Tribal Celebration

The wedding was straight out of *Brides* magazine via Eudora Welty.

My dress was princess-styled white dimity with a hooped skirt and a train; it had dainty lace inserts down the front, a big high Puritan collar, and huge puffed sleeves that came clear to my wrists. My headdress was an organdy Puritan cap that held the white tulle veil in place. I wore white satin shoes and carried into the small white Presbyterian church—which my family had helped to found—a nosegay of white rosebuds and stephanotis.

The bridesmaids wore white dimity dresses, too, with little pink rosebuds all over them, hooped skirts, puffed sleeves, and pink organdy bows in their hair; and they each carried a nosegay of pink rosebuds. The whole family was there, of course, along with everybody else of any importance whatsoever in Hamilton. The local society columnist pulled out all the stops.

My wedding was the culmination of that whole first part of my life; it was also part of a long tradition, which stretched back to my parents' wedding in 1934. What preparations went into it all! What lavish extravagance! My parents could have sent me to the best college in the country for what that wedding cost.

At first I liked the idea of a big Texas wedding, with all the folderol. But I soon realized, *This is really for somebody else. This isn't for me. It has nothing to do with me at all.*

There were endless shopping expeditions with my mother, and sometimes my grandmother as well, to buy a trousseau and a wedding gown and to choose my china and silver. Our tastes were wildly dissimilar and, in the end, someone else decided for me, just as they'd always done. My wedding dress of white dimity was the bridal version of the kinds of clothes Mama liked—clothes I always thought perfectly unsuited to someone with eyeglasses like the bottoms of coke bottles, a freckled face, and an ironing-board figure. At least it had the virtue of being relatively simple.

There were an untold number of showers, given by a whole galaxy of older ladies. They seemed terribly excited by it all, if I wasn't; mostly I was just worn to a frazzle.

The whole ritual wasn't mine; it was manifestly my mother's and my grandmother's. Mine was the chore of remembering who everybody was and what they had given me, thanking them in person and in writing, looking as pretty as I could manage, and smiling, smiling, *smiling*.

The people giving all those parties for me, and those coming to them, weren't even my friends or John's: they were our parents' friends. One college friend and a scattering of old Hamilton schoolmates were the only friends of mine at my own wedding.

It was a great tribal celebration, a ritual rite of passage.

It was also thought to be a fortuitous marriage for all concerned. It was an affirmation to the little town of their values and structure; everyone was so pleased with the match and with our decision to come back to Hamilton to solemnize it: it endorsed the continuity of things. John understood. It was just something to be gotten through, and everyone was happy; he went along, patient and good-hearted: whatever they wanted to do was all right with him.

I was less good-hearted. Through it all—from the big announcement party John's Aunt Nell gave at the country club to the rehearsal dinner his parents held for us, from the shopping trips to selecting the wedding cake smothered in pink and white roses—I tried to ignore my doubts. I pretended to be grown up. I looked grown up and I could act grown up, but I wasn't and I knew I was really faking it. I never quite panicked—but I worried myself half sick.

I remember thinking, *This is a terrible mistake. I can't go through with it. I'm too young.* But I'd had all those parties and people had given me all those tons of presents, and my parents had gone through so much planning and expense . . .

I was publicly committed.

There was no real reason, none I could see as acceptable, to have any doubts about it. And yet . . .

There was no way out.

Was this the *real* reason for such an elaborate wedding, for all the ritual? It locked you in.

*This is the day I'm going to get married*, I thought when I woke the morning of July 1st. *Boy, is this ever a bad idea!*

I thought about the parties and presents, and about the rehearsal we'd had the night before, about everyone's joy and excitement. It had seemed like an elaborate game, like getting ready for a school play. But now it was something else. I began to get anxious, my stomach had a strange knot in it. I didn't want to get out of bed. I wanted to lie in the big oak bed in my grandmother's front bedroom, feel the breeze flutter the summer counterpane, and stare at the pearly flicks on the ceiling wallpaper forever. I didn't want to get up at all. Not ever. Maybe, like the ladies used to do when life got to be too much for them, I could just Go into a Decline.

I thought: *There is absolutely no way I can get out of this. No way. And it's forever.*

We had planned an evening wedding, to avoid the killing July Texas heat. I summoned up the energy and courage to throw off the counterpane; it would be a long day.

Mam-Ma had such a swarm of people at her house that, when it came time to dress in the late afternoon, I went next door to Aunt Eleanor's. I didn't put on my dress because it had been carefully pressed and could not be sat in. Mama spent hours pressing it herself. My great-uncle, who owned the local Cadillac agency, furnished us with a whole fleet of new cars. My immense, fragile dress went to the Presbyterian church in its own Cadillac; my uncle sent a gold car especially for me.

The sun had gone down but it was still hotter than a two-dollar pistol outside. I didn't feel it. I was cold all over. I grew more nervous every minute. It was still light when we drove to the church, and I saw John as we passed by the main entrance, standing outside, talking to an old boyfriend of mine; or at least I think that's who it was. My ugly glasses had to be left off for the occasion so I missed some of the details.

The little church was very simply, beautifully decorated with flowers—and completely packed.

I had been hurt that my own father wouldn't come, but I suppose he thought it was my mother's affair and didn't want to intrude. But other family was everywhere. My cousin Pam was my maid-of-honor, and John's sister Ellen a bridesmaid; two other cousins of mine were flower girls, my brother and a Hamilton boyhood friend of John's were his attendants.

My stepfather gave me away. When we started down the aisle, he tried to make a small joke to cheer me up: "Well, I hope you realize this is the end of your allowance."

I tried to smile but my knees were shaking so I was worried about simply being able to walk. This was very serious. And scary. And *forever*.

A neighbor of my grandmother's played the organ and I had asked the man (John's best man's father) who sang at Mama's wedding to sing the same songs for me. His voice wasn't all it used to be.

When I got up to the altar I started shaking so badly I thought I was going to faint. I wondered seriously if I could make it through this ordeal alive. John had to hold me up. When asked, "Who gives this woman?" Papa kissed me on the cheek and said, "I do." He stepped aside, John said he would take me, and it was over.

We headed directly for the country club, in our fleet of Cadillacs, about five hundred of us, and a long, rambunctious party ensued. I remember standing in the receiving line with John, our families, and the wedding party. Underneath my wedding gown, my white-lace waist-cincher (which made my middle at least two inches smaller by severe pinching) hurt, my high-heeled satin pumps were too tight, the petticoats and the starched dress scratched, it was hotter than a depot stove, and I was muffled up, laced, and miserably uncomfortable.

But it was a genuinely festive affair.

Someone started to play the piano, everyone began to sing, and one uncle spiked the champagne punch with Everclear. Some of my younger cousins got knee-walking drunk. The celebration lasted most of the night, and was remembered and talked about for years.

But long before it was over, John and I escaped. He had gone through elaborate precautions to protect his car from the traditional desecrations; for three days it had been hidden in the sheriff's garage, and at the penultimate moment delivered by a trusted friend.

We drove that night to Austin, stopping every so often for cold Seven-Ups to add to our vodka. We stayed several days at a posh motor inn. It was a lovely honeymoon. We had saved up for a good long while, and we had spent the past few weeks just pleasing other people. We spent the whole time in bed.

And that was very pleasant.

# Two

## John's Wife

# 5

## "No Pockets on Shrouds"

Nothing in my Hamilton childhood had prepared me for my first year of marriage.

It was not exactly what I had expected—not at all.

We lived for the first few months after the wedding in a lovely little house in San Antonio that we rented from a professor on sabbatical. It was clean, quiet, and close to the park and the river—so close to the zoo that we could hear the lions roar in the mornings, and close enough to the river to subject us to a population of enormous water roaches, fully two inches long. Still, those months were close to idyllic.

But we couldn't stay in that house for very long; the professor and his family sold it. And our next place gave me some sobering shocks: we rented what had been the maid's quarters of a big old house in the Castle Hills section of San Antonio. It was a one-room apartment, on an alley, with Salvation Army decor, and a bed that folded out of the wall.

I started back to school that fall, at the only school we could afford, San Antonio Junior College. John, who was teaching at a local high school, registered for his graduate classes at Trinity University, where the tuition was ruinously high—three thousand dollars a year, even then. So I also worked, first for the president of the college and then as a staff artist for the promotion department of the *Light*, the local evening newspaper. The job paid a big two-fifty an hour, which seemed like riches to me; but it was part-time and scarcely made a dent in our burgeoning debts. I quickly learned that commercial art was not for me, and soon fell into the job of writing stories about which newspaper boy collected the most subscriptions and won the company prizes. That suited me much better.

I also began to type John's papers for him—why, I'm not sure. He had taught typing in the Army and was a far better typist than I. Soon I had not only John's papers but those of a friend of his as well. There was my own school work, too. Then, if all that got done, I'd do the housework.

All the housework.

I can remember vividly one day in November, every minute of it. I didn't want to get out of bed that morning, so I didn't. The time for my classes passed and then finally, at noon, I got up and dressed and called the paper to tell my boss I wouldn't be coming in that afternoon. Just making the phone call exhausted what little energy I had. I excused myself by thinking I should stay home and clean up the apartment, but I was just too tired and depressed to do anything at all.

All that afternoon I looked at my wedding pictures.

I remember sitting at the little table looking at the unwashed dishes and the photographs of everyone in pretty dresses and tuxedoes, and wondering, perhaps for the first time, what I had gotten myself into—it was beginning to look like something of a shuck.

Going to school all morning, working all afternoon and part of the early evening, then rushing home to get dinner, to study, to do some cleaning on the house, was burning me out. I needed a breather. I could hardly drag myself around.

I went back to bed, taking the album of wedding pictures with me. Would we ever get that photographer paid off? John had ordered the man to take pictures like there was no tomorrow, never asking how much they would cost. We owed him over a hundred dollars; it might have been a million for all I knew about where we'd find that kind of money.

I looked at them slowly, page by page. There I was in my wedding gown, and John in his dinner jacket. There were pictures of all the aunts and uncles, the cousins, my mother and stepfather, John's parents. There I was, feeding John a slice of wedding cake. Everyone dressed up fit to kill, everyone smiling and happy. John and I happy. As we ran out of the country club together, John and I were laughing with joy . . .

I looked around our tacky little room. I had begun to paint the kitchen, when I could find the time; the rest badly needed painting, too. The furniture that had come with the place—a couch and chair with wagon-wheel arms and upholstery featuring steers and horses—I had pronounced "early raunch" and banished to the landlord's garage; I preferred living with little furniture to being forced to look at things so ugly.

The place was a farunctious mess. Tired after dinner the night before, I'd left the dishes in the old sink and fallen asleep over a French translation. The trash hadn't been carried out, either, and the floor was so dirty that walking barefoot was a hazard.

I felt like crying, but lacked the energy even for that. Anyway, what excuse did I have for crying? Could it be so hard? I should just pull myself together and get it done. *It's supposed to be my job, after all. But still . . . but still . . . John lives here too, and has less to do than I do. Would it kill him to give me a hand?*

He couldn't understand that. His mother had always taught school and kept house, his father took care of the yard.

My mother had either done all the housework herself or had supervised others who did it. The only man I'd ever seen do dishes or clean was our Japanese houseboy.

Why was I getting so upset about something as trivial and dumb as *housework?* That was John's question, and so it was mine, too. Just as I wasn't supposed to mind doing it, I wasn't supposed to question why it all fell to me, either.

I had no way of dealing, that year, with all the small, subtle conflicts that naturally arise when you're trying to work out just living with someone else for the first time. I'd never seen my parents argue, and I didn't know how to argue myself. Scenes of any kind, even the slightest bit of unpleasantness, made me sick at my stomach. So John and I had no real confrontations. I assumed that he would take care of me, and couldn't believe that he was capable of taking advantage of me as well. Any protest or objection I made was always delivered in such a small voice, it's no wonder he never heard.

I felt flashes of resentment toward John, which I could neither express nor reconcile with loving him so very much.

I had always idealized John, with that special worship I tended to give to people who were older, who knew things I wanted to know. But one of the few things I began to understand that day was that my hero worship of him was beginning to slip—just as I'm sure the pedestal he had put me on had gotten a little shorter, too. *Still*, I thought, *dirty socks smell bad.*

When he came home that evening I could see that he resented me for not having done "my" work, and I can remember resenting his resentment.

But I also felt guilty, damned guilty. Millions of other women did it, didn't they?

Something magical happened to me the next year, something that's happened to a lot of people in their second or third year of college. You find yourself in a course, and suddenly everything falls together. And it all makes sense. That's how I felt when we moved to Denton.

We made the move because John had finished his master's degree and decided to work on his doctorate at North Texas State. I could return to TSCW; and after a year at the junior college, Tessie didn't seem like such a bad place after all. John still had his GI Bill; we could get college housing, so it would be cheaper than living in San Antonio.

I didn't care about not having any money. We had made a lot of new friends in Denton, mostly couples going to school on the GI Bill, too, and everybody was in the same boat. We helped each other, shared meals, and whatever luxuries we had—clothes for special occasions, beer and spaghetti when the government checks arrived. And anyway, I was too caught up in what was happening finally to my brain at school to worry about it.

Art history and philosophy were the magical courses for me. I'd always been interested in art; but art history was all new to me. To my surprise, reading and talking about art were much more interesting than *making* it. My medieval course was exciting and fascinating. To discover that art wasn't just a picture of something, or even just some sort of image, but that it was an *idea*, that it could incorporate whole sets of ideas that could be read like a code once you learned to decipher it—that wiped me out. I had a very good teacher. "You have to travel, you have to get out and see the real things," she'd tell us. "Slides can only *remind* you." Now that I was learning how to look, would I ever get out of dumb old Texas again and see something?

She taught me other things, too. She taught me the joy of knowing something well, of mastering a discipline. I had enjoyed a sense of power in Kyoto, when my boyfriend and I were running most of everything at the high school; this was a new kind of power, over a subject and oneself, and it was infinitely more satisfying.

And yet, for all my enthusiasm, hard work, and good grades, I am appalled and puzzled that I didn't learn to read or think critically until so much later. Perhaps it was the strangely docile world of a girls' school in the fifties. The girls would sit in class and knit. A professor could have said, "The world is coming to an end tomorrow," and they'd have put down their needles, made a careful note, and then picked up their knitting again.

I'd always felt competitive with boys and then men. I had some of this feeling toward John. But it was like having an older brother, one who's always bigger and stronger and ahead of you in school.

It was like being on a treadmill: I could never catch up.

John encouraged my sense of competitiveness. He taught me how to shoot, and I became pretty good with a .22 pistol. He always insisted that I come along on his hunting trips, even though I was the only woman. The men had been hunting together for years, and those weekend trips to south Texas, to hunt coon, wildcat, and *javalina*, were male-bonding events of the first order. We'd head off in a station wagon, collecting men and dogs along the way. We had two dogs—a fine old tracking hound named Tonto, and a Black and Tan puppy that was mine. I named him Sam and loved him dearly even though he was as dumb as a Fundamentalist preacher. The men would all sit up front together and I'd ride in the back with the dogs.

I guess they came to look upon me as a kind of mascot, though they were always afraid I'd be trouble to them, or that they'd have to watch their language. But they'd generally forget I was there when the dogs were set loose, and we'd all follow on foot, at a half-run through the heavy brush and chaparral, listening to the dogs running and barking, then running like crazy ourselves when we heard the special hound music that meant a coon had been treed. After that it was only a matter of time before the coon was coaxed or fooled out of the tree, whereupon the dogs would rip it to pieces.

A thoroughly vicious, violent business.

Once a huge forty-pounder jumped down out of an oak tree, landing right on my back, knocking me down: the dogs made the kill on top of me. Fortunately I was wearing a heavy coat. Everybody thought that a marvelous joke. I even got to the point I could laugh about it myself.

Though I learned the routine well enough, my puppy Sam remained incurably stupid. Once, on a wildcat-hunting expedition at a friend's ranch in south Texas, he lit out after some cows. A very jerky guy who sometimes hunted with us picked up a piece of stove wood and took out after my dog, shouting, "I'm gonna break that dog of that."

I grabbed up a piece of stove wood, too, and took after him. "Goddamn you, you leave my dog alone," I hollered, "or I'll part your hair with this!"

I surprised myself as much as I did him and he did drop the log, but I paid for it. All day he teased and baited me, trying to make me quit or break down, and the next morning he asked me if I wanted to go riding with him. It was clearly a dare, but I wasn't afraid; I'd ridden a lot when I was younger. He knew the ranch well, along with its stock, and went off and brought back a horse that looked like it had never even been ridden; it was a really wild, crazy, bad horse; you could see the whites of both its eyes.

I looked over to John, and he showed no expression. He always let me shift for myself, which I liked; he wanted me to come on the hunts, and thought they were good for me. But this guy was clearly trying to get me killed.

"Well?" my tormentor asked.

I looked at the horse again. It was a bad horse, all right—and a squeeze play. But I could simply refuse to play, and I did. Though John and everybody else in the hunting party congratulated me privately on my good sense, I would much rather have been able to ride that crazy horse.

In spite of the bad experiences, I loved those hunting trips; they enabled me to do things that my family had never approved of—masculine things that women from my world weren't supposed to do. The men might not have liked my presence all that much, but I liked being

there, and fighting back and trying to do things just as
well or better than they could—and I think John enjoyed
that spirit in me.

I even didn't much mind staying in the back of the station wagon with the dogs; it was often cold and you
could wrap the dogs around you. It was smelly but warm;
and I could sleep.

Along with our school work, John and I both had jobs
that year. He administered tests for the psychology department and I was a student assistant in the art department. I learned to make slides, which, much later, proved
a handy skill to have. I also lettered diplomas and
plaques—a very medieval occupation but one I enjoyed.
The most bizarre job I had was modeling lingerie for a
local wholesale firm. My boss told me they liked me "because you're wholesome-looking and wear pajamas well"—
but I couldn't see much future in that.

Student labor was both plentiful and cheap in Denton, and our jobs paid us only a pittance—like the forty
cents an hour I got for making slides—and the GI Bill just
wasn't enough for tuition and to live on as well. Our
friends were getting by only because the wives all worked
full-time to help "put hubby through."

John insisted: "I want you to get an education, too." I
wanted it, too—more than ever—but our financial troubles
grew worse. We always owed money to the teacher's
credit union.

What had been fun—being poor together—was becoming a dreadfully serious business. I took a hard look at how
we were living. It seemed clear that if we didn't curb ourselves we'd starve flat damn to death. I wrote out the

checks and had to figure out how we were going to pay for everything. But I was only the purser, not the commodore.

"There are no pockets on shrouds," John used to say.

I loved him for his happy extravagance, but the burden was beginning to tell. Those hunting trips were expensive, school was expensive, an unmaintained car dribbled away hundreds of dollars, and finally, by late that year, we ran out of money.

We'd borrowed all we could; both of us would have to work full-time until we paid off our debts and saved enough to go back to school. Denton didn't provide enough opportunities so we decided to try Dallas. I landed a secretarial job in the personnel department of a large corporation, but John found nothing. Everyone he saw said he had too much education and in too specialized a field for their purposes.

We began to discuss again the obvious and common alternative—I'd work full-time so John could finish his degree. It would be a sacrifice, and frankly I didn't want to make it. I remembered the last summer in San Antonio, which we'd already spent that way; I remembered the resentment I'd felt and the strain it had placed on our marriage. I thought about my friend Kate, who had given up her studies and taken a job as a secretary to get her husband through the university. And I thought of how exhilarated I had been this year by my courses, how much they meant to me now.

But I didn't say any of these things to John.

# 6

## Young Mama

We fell into a lucky situation. A new men's dormitory had been built at North Texas and the administration wanted a married couple to live there and manage it. His wife, they reasoned, would be a civilizing influence. Meals would be furnished, along with a free and pleasant apartment; there would even be a small salary to supplement John's teaching assistantship. And I could continue going to school.

It looked like the beginning of good times.

That year I began to wonder what I was going to do with myself. What *could* I do? I mean, what skills did I have? Not many.

Primarily I was "John's wife." I was glad to be that, I had chosen to be that, but it didn't require quite all of my time and energy. And what if, God forbid, something should happen to him? The job I had in the art department, even though it was full-time, certainly didn't pay enough to support myself.

I tried to learn shorthand, but I'd look at all those dumb

symbols and go blind. Shorthand was the first course I failed.

I was the only one worried about my lack of career; friends and parents were beginning to ask why John and I hadn't started a family. We'd been married over two years, was anything wrong? We had already begun thinking about it ourselves.

Kathleen was a very much planned and much wanted child. I was delighted when I learned I was pregnant; so was John. Our parents were thrilled. But something was very odd about my pregnancy. I not only had morning sickness, but all-day-long and all-night-long sickness. I threw up all the time. At work. In the apartment. In the ladies' room across the hall from my art history class, which I was forced to flee daily about ten minutes into the lecture. That class was in a pseudo-Georgian building with polished marble everywhere, bathrooms included. My daily dash to flash the hash was clearly audible to everybody on the first floor of the art building.

Was it all connected to a fear of having a child? If so, it had to be an unconscious fear.

John, who was always good to me in so many ways, became even more solicitous; he fetched my coffee, lit my cigarettes, took me to the local Mexican restaurant once a week. The woman I had chosen as my obstetrician was less sympathetic, however. Even though she practiced in Dallas, I had gone to Dr. Fuller because she *was* a woman; I appreciated women professionals and identified strongly with them. The respect wasn't mutual.

She was one of those women who have, with great difficulty, transcended being a woman and become an honorary man.

She had no patience with me or my troubles. I guess

other women just served to remind her that she couldn't escape being one of us, after all. Her response to illness—and pregnancy *was* an illness to her—was that I'd snap out of it.

I didn't.

I continued sick and miserable, and that frightened me: I'd always heard that pregnancy was a beautiful experience.

Everything I'd ever learned about the first stages of motherhood was positive propaganda; all the negative aspects had been glossed over or censored. It was only after I was irrevocably committed to becoming a mother that the conspiracy of silence ended. Now other women came forward to sympathize with me about all the discomforts and to regale me with horror stories. I carefully put out of my mind the ones about actually giving birth, and tried to concentrate on the immediate problem of keeping food down me long enough to prevent me and my baby from dying of malnutrition.

The doctor was pleased with me about only one thing: I wasn't gaining any weight. I was losing it. When I complained to her that I was still nauseated all the time, even after the first few months, she informed me that I had to be exaggerating—nobody could be sick all that much. One of John's aunts, a nurse, was furious that nothing was being done. Actually, I was taking anti-upchuck pills, but nothing would stay put in my stomach long enough to help. My mother-in-law called from San Antonio every other day, the dormitory dietitian worked overtime dreaming up special treats for me, the boys in the dorm even worried.

My body didn't even seem to belong to me anymore. It didn't look like mine and it was certainly behaving very badly.

I spared my mother, who was in Germany, the details. That was one small favor to be thankful for—she was far enough away not to have to know what was going on.

In my seventh month, it all came to an end. I woke up one night convinced that the time—though it was much too soon—had come.

I kept imagining Fuller's displeasure at being awakened at three A. M., but finally I called her. She wasn't the least persuaded, told me to go on to the hospital if it would pleasure me—I'd just have to come home in the morning.

That was our last difference of opinion: I delivered Kathleen the next morning. Six weeks premature, she weighed only three pounds, four-and-a-half ounces, and had red hair, a tiny head, and very skinny legs. They put her into an isolette immediately. I was delighted to have done with the business in such a hurry, and to have her there, healthy and whole, though in miniature.

I felt shock and relief at having my own body back so suddenly, and had the satisfaction of knowing that I had given birth with very little sedation, with little difficulty. I decided that pregnancy and childbirth weren't so bad after all, that I could see myself through the next time, and I wanted there to be a next time soon. And next time I wouldn't rely on a lot of faulty information.

I laughed at one of my artist friends who came to the hospital to congratulate me on "that most creative of all experiences." Whoever dreamed up and perpetuated that notion *had* to be male. I was only the hostess for the event. Everything took place in secret, dark inside of me, without my thought or control. I was inside the myth and mystery now and I could laugh.

As I think back to those first days of Kathleen's life, it is hard to remember what I really felt about her and what I thought I was supposed to feel. I felt pleased and relieved, of course, glad that she was healthy and strong. I remember being upset that I couldn't even hold her until she was nearly a month old, or nurse her—as I'd so much wanted to do. Twice a day I'd go to the hospital to look at her, listening to others, who would spot Kathleen and say, "Oh, how tiny!" or once, "Ain't she pee-tight!"

She was an enormous pleasure to me. I loved to watch her; everything she did enchanted me. We'd sit on the floor together, or on a bed, and play—sometimes with the marvelous pink cow my Aunt Tink had given her, a stuffed toy with a red felt tongue sticking out and a funny little udder. Kathleen slept with it, played with it, and as soon as she could talk, she named it "Moo." It got grubby pretty quickly, and when I'd put it in the washing machine, she'd watch through the glass as it turned round and round, and then followed it to the dryer, to be sure ole Moo came out all right.

Though her advent did change it radically, we never let Kathleen dominate our life. She went almost everywhere with us. We took her to picnics at the lake, where John and a friend or two would fish for crappie and perch while I sat under a tree and read or played with Kathleen. She'd sit on my lap when people came over to play bridge. John had to be at the dormitory, so at home, virtually all the time in those years, and Kathleen's care was shared almost equally; John liked taking care of her, he liked playing with her, and he liked being with her.

There were always lots of people around Kathleen— people who loved her. She was held and cuddled so much it's a wonder her skin didn't rub off.

My friend Wendy brought her a couple of Van Gogh prints, because babies like to look at bright things, and we put those up in her room. And I always dressed her in brightly colored clothes, because I didn't care much for the traditional pink and blue.

What a delightful, untroublesome baby she was! Happy and outgoing, she would start the day chuckling and chortling. We had a little game: as soon as she'd hear me coming in for her, she'd stop her noises, lie down, and pretend to be asleep. "All right," I'd say, "you don't want to get up yet." No change in her position. "Well, I think I'll just go back to sleep again." And then she'd jump up and laugh, stretching out her little fat arms for her morning hug.

She was the pet of the dorm. Everyone played with her, and she was much made over by the boys who lived in the dormitory. When she was big enough to get around by herself, she'd wander out of our apartment and into the lounge. For a time, she and some of the athletes would watch the *Mickey Mouse Club* on TV together. They'd all sit there religiously, Kathleen and her hulking jock buddies, singing "M-I-C, K-E-Y . . ." But John and I disapproved of television, and she knew it. Or maybe she just got bored with Mickey Mouse. She not only abandoned the set, she began to harass the still-devoted viewers, racing past on her tricycle, shaking her fist and sternly announcing: "You're rotting your minds!"

I usually dressed her in T-shirts and overalls, and she'd play with trucks as readily as with dolls. A psychology major in the dorm made a big point of telling me I was confusing her "role association," but I never worried about such things, thought it was trivial. I only wanted her to have toys she'd be happy with, to wear clothes that would be practical and comfortable—and that I wouldn't have to iron. In fact, she enjoyed playing with *things* more than with toys—empty tin cans and milk cartons that she'd turn into play-things, and the pieces of John's chess set, which she often mislaid.

She seemed to have a minimum number of the problems mentioned in my well-thumbed copy of Dr. Spock—perhaps because we treated her with a kind of benevolent neglect. She never cried at night; when I'd put her to bed, she'd go right to sleep. She wasn't toilet-trained very early, because Dr. Spock had warned me we were in for a struggle, so I kept putting it off from one school vacation to the next. Finally, she was two and I was thoroughly sick of the diaper drill, so I simply said, "Look, Beano, most people go to the potty instead of using diapers. Don't you think it would be a nice idea if you tried it?" So she tried it—and she liked it.

I started back to school again when she was six months old, intent on finishing my interminable BA. John was always home, so we didn't have a babysitting problem; still, having Kathleen around made studying much more difficult. I was nearing the end of my undergraduate work, majoring in history at North Texas now, and had an immense amount of reading to do and a lot of papers to write. It was hard to find concentrated chunks of time for myself, except late at night, but I was determined to finish.

There were few women in the history department and we were discouraged, sometimes subtly, sometimes flagrantly. One American history prof told me flatly: "American history is definitely not a woman's field; try European." The European man told me just the reverse.

The apartment was piled high with my books and John's books. Kathleen couldn't have liked all our studying and reading very much, because once, when she was about two-and-a-half, she did one of the few really naughty things I can remember from those years. When I came in to get her up after her nap one afternoon, she'd torn the pages out of fully two-thirds of her books.

Soon after she could talk she devised some imaginary playmates, who remained with us for several months, and who prompted me to visit with other young mamas on campus so Kathleen would have some friends who were neither imaginary nor athletes with rotting minds. There were Goo, Lou, Lee, and Posto Flake. The latter was very small and very good. The others were pure evil. They would do all the things she wasn't supposed to do, and if she was ever blamed for something, it was always Goo or Lou or Lee who'd done the dirty deed, not Kathleen.

She was mischievous and inquisitive at times and she also liked to declare her independence. Stubbornly. When she was three-and-a-half, my mother-in-law convinced me that she should start learning to read, and that the best way to do this was with flash cards.

"Now, this is a B, Kathleen," I said, holding it up before her eyes.

She looked at it very solemnly and said: "No, it's a Q."

"No," I corrected her, "it's a B."

"No, it's a Q."

"It's a B!"

"Q."

"Damnit, Kathleen," I said. "I've got a college degree, and I *know* the stupid alphabet! If I say this is a B, then it *is* a B!"

But I got nowhere at all, and realized that though I might someday be able to teach something to somebody, my own daughter wasn't going to learn to read from me.

Those were happy years for me. I made friends easily

and soon we amassed a circle of very stimulating people. My best friend was Glenda, whom I'd met in a history class. She seemed to me to be so marvelous I could hardly believe she'd want to be friends with me. She was a graduate student, and not only bright as a dollar but terrifically funny as well. We enjoyed each other's company, especially because both of us loved to tell the stories we'd both grown up on—little-town southern stories. It takes another yarner to appreciate them to the fullest, and Glenda was superb. Timpson, Texas, was her mother lode, and neither of us ever ran short. And if we did, the weekly local papers from both towns would remind us of something.

Glenda was teaching two freshman classes for the department and finishing her master's degree. She was my age but unmarried.

I was dumbfounded when she decided to become a bride; and part of that surprise was at myself for not being delighted about it. After all, wasn't I the best example I knew of wedded bliss? Of course I was! I never thought anything else for a single minute. Then why did it seem to me as though Glenda didn't truly appreciate what she was giving up? Marriage was okay for *me*, but . . .

But I was no Glenda. I thought she had everything—not only intelligence and wit and talent, but she was blond and pretty as a picture on the wall, and from a fairly well-to-do family as well. The life she was leading as a single, independent graduate student seemed ideal. She didn't need someone to take care of her the way I did; she could take care of herself. She even had her own apartment! If she had the sense God gave a rubber duck, she wouldn't throw it all away like that.

But she did it anyway, and all I could do was shake my

head and wish her even more happiness than it seemed to me she was so wantonly abandoning.

We saw Glenda and her husband often, we played bridge, and we went to parties at the lake, where, until the wee hours of the morning, everybody talked and talked.

We also went to church regularly. I had been taken only sporadically as a child and it had never been very important to me. Thinking that perhaps I'd missed something, soon after Kathleen was born I decided to try it again. Church would provide her, at least until she began to question it, with an explanation of the world and a code of behavior. If and when that wore out, she'd have a foundation within the institution from which to question it intelligently. The church we attended in Denton was small and friendly, and John and the rector became good friends. I kept active in parish doings, not only there, but in all the places we lived. To do that was simply part of my responsibility to my family, rather than to God. The liturgy, the music, were beautiful and satisfying in and of themselves. The magic, mystical, mysterioso qualities appealed to me greatly.

As Kathleen grew, so did her material needs.

And I began to have a strange, haunting fear that something would happen to John. Sometimes, in the night, I'd wake up and touch his chest gently to see if he was still breathing. *I need him. I can't get along without him.*

I began to brood over what I'd do if something ever took him from me. How could I support us? Stenography was out, of course, since I couldn't learn the damned hieroglyphics; and I knew I'd need at least an MA, which would take me years and years, in order to teach.

I was willing to try anything. "What you ought to do is learn how to fly," a friend of ours told me one day, when I was worrying out loud about the problem. "Then you could be a crop-duster."

"*A crop-duster?*"

"Sure. It doesn't take very much time, you wouldn't have to be away from Kathleen much, and it pays like a busted slot machine."

I couldn't argue with that kind of logic and right away began flying lessons. My teacher had a little Piper Cub, and the instructions progressed for quite a while. I really began to enjoy flying enormously. Finally we started on the hard part. Hedge-hopping. Flying down rivers. Flying close to the ground. You can't dust crops at five thousand feet.

Part of the problem was that I still really didn't see very well. I didn't have contact lenses then, and with my glasses had very little peripheral vision. We'd flown down a river bed one day and I started hedge-hopping. On the second dip, the plane zoomed under a telephone wire that was strung from a pole to a house, and I clipped it with the propeller blade. I heard it snap. So did my instructor.

As soon as I'd put a little more air between us and the ground, he motioned me to bring the plane in. He didn't need to argue. I made the usual two runs, rather shakily, to drive off the cow population, and then landed on the Denton Municipal Airport runway. When the plane had come to a full stop, he said in a hoarse whisper: "*Do you realize how close we came to dying?*"

"Yes, I do," I said.

He said, "Well, I just don't think I can handle this any more, Judy. You understand."

That was the end of my flying career.

When Kathleen was two years old, I was pregnant again. But I started spotting and then bleeding after three

months and had to take to the bed. Soon afterward I had
my first miscarriage.

Within six months I was pregnant again. It was something of a surprise, but not necessarily an unhappy one.

I had finally almost finished my BA at North Texas,
had a happy, healthy child of two, so was less fearful, less
self-absorbed than I'd been when I carried Kathleen. But
midway in my fourth month I started to bleed again and
had to spend a great deal of time in bed.

Late one afternoon, while I was thick into a book on
high Renaissance art, I felt the baby stop moving. I went
to the doctor, who listened and ran some tests. Several
days later the results came back. The baby was dead.

"What happens now?" I asked.

"We'll just have to wait."

"Can't you do something?" I asked in amazement. The
thought of carrying the baby any longer upset and frightened me.

"No," he said. "It's much better if this happens naturally."

John was very indulgent and worried about what it was
doing to me; for the next month and a half I felt like a
walking coffin.

I did everything I could think of to induce labor, short
of throwing myself down a flight of stairs. Then, in the
sixth month, I began labor and delivered.

They never told me whether my baby was a boy or girl.
Because I was an obstetrical case of a sort, I was kept in
the maternity ward of the hospital, where all the other
women had successfully delivered their children. Often
nurses would come around to distribute the babies to be
fed, and I can remember several who popped smiling faces
into my room and asked: "Where's your baby, dear?"

When I got out, I plunged myself into school work, finished my BA and began graduate school, majoring in art history. In time I gradually felt my ambition to have any more children fade away. Other things occupied my mind.

# 7

## "What If
## Kathleen Should
## Marry One?"

In 1959 the civil rights movement came to Denton. It was my first major political commitment. It was also the beginning of independence for me, because John and I did not agree about it. I had always followed his lead in political matters, offering advice when asked for; now I took the initiative.

John *wanted* to become involved. He shared most of my views. But he felt that because he worked for the administration, on the dean of men's staff, and because he was still finishing his doctorate—which wasn't going well, not at all—he'd have to act out his commitment in other ways. A public display of protest struck him as both ineffectual and even dangerous.

I could not resist it.

There was great visible discrimination around the campus. The school itself had not been integrated very long; none of the restaurants would serve blacks; the movies admitted them only to the balconies; there were separate restrooms and water fountains everywhere—and Jim Crow sections in the railroad and bus stations.

Denton had sit-ins and demonstrations, and we'd all stand in line together at the movie house singing songs. There was some trouble and the police, at times, got pretty rough, but Denton didn't have the confrontations so common in other parts of the South that year. It seemed to me that no matter what happened, good or bad, Texas got a watered-down version. Still, I loved the involvement, the danger and the planning—loved the feeling that I was in on something important, something that was *right*. It was exciting and it was fun. Glenda was up to her chin in it, too, and that made me all the more confident of what I was doing.

On vacations, I began to get into serious discussions with some of my more traditionally disposed relations. "What if Kathleen should want to *marry* one?" Nobody ever believed me when I shrugged my shoulders.

When my father, at a large family dinner, announced, "I know what it is to be oppressed," thinking probably of his days as a Brother Rat, I lost my temper completely. "Bullshit!" I shouted. "You've never been oppressed in your life! All you know about oppression is how to commit it—you *own* the world!"

That was just too much, I'd gone too far. But lightning didn't strike. There was an uncomfortable silence.

"Mercy!" murmured Aunt Mag, fanning herself with her hand and looking pale.

"Well, there are just some things we don't talk about with Judy at the dinner table," Aunt Belle, the hostess, calmly announced. She was obviously distressed, but hiding it well. "One of them is the Nee-grow problem."

Until I went to college, I had never known a Negro who was not a servant or a menial of some kind. Those I had known best were people who worked for us, and I had been especially fond of a driver named Snuffy, who was my father's right hand for many years, and several women who had been with the family for long periods of time.

I came into the movement through white friends, and at first there wasn't too much mixing. Then, as we all became more and more involved, there began to be parties. Mixed parties. The first I'd ever gone to. I remember with stark vividness the first time I ever danced with a Negro. Terror, exhilaration, and just plain mischief all combined. I thought: *My God, if my grandfather could see me now he would positively rotate in his grave. My mother would just plain kill me.*

It was so pathetic. Everyone was trying so hard to make contact, and there was such an impossible gulf between us. My hair was very long at the time, and as we danced the young man gently touched it. "God," he said quietly, "your hair is just so soft."

I didn't have the nerve to touch his.

It had never been forbidden expressly. Relations with Negroes, of any kind other than master-servant, was, quite simply, beyond my reckoning. I had never been aware that it ever *could* happen. But it was happening, and the experience was tremendously electric even if it didn't always work.

While John and I differed, and began to grow farther apart because of my increasing involvement, the pressure grew from other sources as well. My brother, three of my cousins, and John's sister were in school in Denton too; we'd been a solid family—but civil rights began to divide us. One professor, whom I'd admired very much—thinking him a sympathetic, brilliant man, and a great liberal—called Glenda and me into his office one day and said:

"You should really think about what you're doing!" He advised us that not only could we get ourselves in trouble but we were endangering our husbands' careers, even their degrees.

But I could not stop.

I'd always been interested in governmental politics, particularly the Byzantine intrigue of Texas politics; I had loved my Texas government class, which everyone warned me was dull enough to put you in a coma. I'd been interested in the Kennedy campaign and had helped organize the precincts. But civil rights was a real issue; it was deeper, more immediate, more personal. The injustice was clear.

John never told me not to do anything. He did not approve of my methods but, just as on those hunting trips, I had to do what I had to do, he insisted. I could see that I was getting deeper into a bind; I knew both sides—the administration's, from John; the protestors', because I was one and knew where the meetings and demonstrations were going to be held and who would be taking part in them. And what made me so uneasy and increased the distance between us, was that I couldn't share with John the events that were so important to me.

The president of the college, whom I saw at college social functions, would pat me on the head and speak lightly about my activities, as if to say: "Aren't you having fun?" John often didn't seem to take my commitment very seriously either, and that made me angry. If what I was doing wasn't important, why did everyone get so upset at other times about my doing it?

We did some good. We integrated the movie houses and the cafes around the campus, and I had the selfish satisfaction of knowing I was doing something *I* wanted to do—

and that I was being effective at it. But I remember some harrowing experiences. We were roughed up and pushed around, several young professors lost their jobs, and a few in the group went to jail. Once another history major—a black guy—and I went together to a place called Jake's House to see if we would be served. It was a crumby old soda fountain place nobody ever went to anyway, but we went in and sat down at the counter together. The man behind the counter treated us to fifteen minutes' worth of Hate Stare, and when that didn't work, reached under the counter, pulled out a .45, and placed the business end about two inches away from my nose. "You and that god-damn nigger get out of here," he said between his teeth, "and don't you ever come back!"

We didn't stay.

John had been finishing his course work and working sporadically on his dissertation, a statistical study of administrative theory and philosophy. It involved hundreds of tiresome questionnaires, and he went into the doldrums over it. Then the worst happened. Someone published a similar study. His whole dissertation, which meant so much to our lives, went right out from under him and shrank to one chapter. That was all the material he could salvage.

Living in the dorm drove him deeper into a stalemate. There were constant interruptions. The phone rang all day, and half the night someone was always knocking on the door, or coming in drunk and disorderly, or playing some prank, like putting a dead skunk into the air-conditioning system.

He decided he would be better off getting a full-time job. This time there was no question of my continued schooling. I had a college degree and I had a baby to take care of. It was time we addressed ourselves to getting John's career off the ground.

So I dropped out of graduate school, said reluctant good-byes to all my friends in Denton, especially Glenda—and we moved back to San Antonio. John signed on as the vice-principal of a large junior high school.

I had spent two of the worst years of my life in San Antonio: but they proved far less than adequate preparation for the disastrous year that lay ahead.

# 8

## "Be Happy in Your Work"

Less than three months after we moved to San Antonio I went bananas.

I began to mislay my mind, almost lost it completely. I became narcoleptic, I began to cry all day, I wouldn't leave the house or answer the phone; I even made futile threats to kill myself. Which was ridiculous as well as unnecessary. Because I was *already* dead.

Betty Friedan wrote about "the problem that has no name" in 1963. This was a little too late for me. Like thousands of women who never know what's happening to them, I had it—in spades. I couldn't understand what was wrong, and felt guilty as hell because my life, to all outward appearances, was no different and scarcely worse than that of thousands of other women. Feeling guilty of course only compounded the problem.

What *was* happening to me?

Why was I *sure* I was dead?

Before we bought our own house, where it all happened, we lived with John's parents in San Antonio for a

few months. It shouldn't have been so bad. Certainly the
house was big enough, and I had always loved the Sullivans; they were bright, well-read, interesting, and fun.
They also happened to be conservative Republicans, and
Daddy was precinct chairman for the local Goldwater
campaign that year; he had Goldwater signs all over the
front yard, and we had political arguments at the dinner
table. John's sister Ellen, who had spent all her summers with us from the time we married until she did, was
also living at home with her new husband. He teased
both Ellen and Kathleen until they cried—I despised
him wholeheartedly, thought he was a waste of fresh air
and orange juice, told him so often, and we had bitter,
frequent fights.

When September came, everyone headed off to school
or work—John, his parents, Ellen, and her husband. Everyone but me and Kathleen. Stuck without a car, ten
miles from even the nearest shopping center, I suddenly
found myself isolated and bored. And since we were staying there, and I was there at home, the least I could do, I
thought, was the housework. So I cleaned house, washed,
ironed, cooked, and shopped for the whole household. By
this time I'd learned something about how it was all done.
I was even getting crazy about it: not crazy-joyful but
crazy-compulsive.

John had to put in twelve- to fifteen-hour days at the
school, which upset Kathleen—who loved being with him
as I did. I kept thinking of the good old days in Denton—
missing my friends, especially Glenda, but most of all,
wishing we had our own place again. Whenever I could,
Kathleen and I would brave the 108-degree heat on house-
hunting expeditions until we were both too hot and cross
to stand it anymore. Then we'd go back and begin the big

dinner that usually turned into a political argument or a fight with Ellen's husband.

The strain began to get to me. I became tense as a piano wire, often sick at my stomach, and my forehead broke out in clear blisters.

So as soon as we could, we bought and moved into a small new house about ten blocks north of the folks, the first place of our own.

It was a pretty little house, with pink brick in front and white shutters and siding, in a housing development where every third house repeated itself and tried hard not to look like it. All the houses for six blocks in that hilly, northern area of San Antonio were owned by families about our age, with young children, and everybody there earned eight to twelve thousand dollars a year. Up and down the block, a few stubby trees, newly planted, struggled to get a toehold in the dry, rocky soil; the front lawns got grass gratis from the developer, the back lawns came bare. People were forever planting all sorts of things, but they seemed so slow to grow.

After we'd paid the closing costs, bought a washer, refrigerator, two beds and new clothes for John—he was in a responsible position, and one suit wouldn't cut it anymore—we had reached the limit of our credit. The rest of our furniture was the same old early Salvation Army stuff, which I had painted and repainted every time we moved.

Still, it was a big step from the alley we'd lived on when we first lived in San Antonio. *We'll fix it up,* I thought, *and it will start to look like we want it to.* And it was exciting in the beginning. John worked on the lawn when he could, I put out some bulbs and planted ivy in the front. The little spindly trees would grow, the ivy would flourish, we'd have a home.

I tried desperately to get that ivy to take hold, but the sun was just too hot; all my optimism shriveled up right along with it.

Perhaps it was the women. They all seemed a little out of whack. One drank too much, another was hooked on TV; there was even a religious fanatic. I was walking up the street one day to fetch Kathleen home for her nap, and passed one of my neighbors working in her flower beds. She was crying her eyes out. *Bawling.*

"What's wrong, Imogene? For heaven sakes, is there anything I can do?" I asked, startled.

She looked up and without preamble said: "Sex, sex, sex. That's all he ever thinks about is *sex!* Why can't he just leave me alone?"

Jean, who lived across the street, had four children, the youngest a baby and the oldest just six. She seemed locked in a vicious cycle that was draining everything human from her. She was overweight and hooked on Pepsi Cola. She never spoke to her children; she yelled at them. She stayed up most of the night, every night, ironing and doing housework, watching whatever was on television; then she slept most of the next day. Her husband would feed the children breakfast and push them out the door before he went to work. Jean got up around noon, fed the kids, then almost always came over to my house, let herself in, and planted herself at the card table that was passing for our dining-room furniture. There she'd proceed to tell me in minute detail, first everything that had been on the tube the night before, then all the intimate details of her sex life.

I didn't want to hear any of it; I had my own TV set, my own sex life, and work to do. But I couldn't get rid of her; I felt too sorry for her to be rude.

I began to spend a lot more time with Jean than I really wanted to, simply because she appeared every day and I didn't have the gumption to run her off. I had been used to Glenda and other friends who were doing interesting things and who talked about ideas, events out in the world. Now even Glenda was having her problems; they, too, had left Denton and she was stuck in a boring, crazy-making job to put her husband through his PhD while her own career went by the boards.

Jean and I talked about the only things we had in common: the meals we had to shop for and fix; the money that was never quite sufficient to make ends meet no matter how we scrimped and saved; our houses, our children.

She was as worried, as honestly concerned as I was, about raising her children and making a good home for her family. Yet she was doing a miserable job of it, and I was convinced—and this was increasingly unsettling—that I wasn't doing any better. Nor were any of the women on that block.

The children were strong. They survived. They had a free run of our rather deserted street and ran in herds—the threes, fours, fives, and six-year-olds in a pack. They are all mixed up in my mind now, though God knows I saw a lot of them. All I can remember is being grateful that there weren't any beastly ones in the lot, like those boys down the street from my in-laws who'd throw Kathleen down and stuff her mouth with dirt—or strangle her baby ducks.

Kathleen fixed up a section of our garage to look like a house; it had a little play stove and refrigerator, her doll bed and a few small chairs. From the kitchen, while I sewed or ironed, I could hear the children playing there. Once, when her friend Jimmy drove her toy car into the garage, she said: "Oh, honey! How many times do I have to ask you not to drive the car into the living room?"

God, she had mimicked my very own voice—whining, imploring, convinced the request wouldn't be heard, much less heeded.

I began to see in Kathleen reflections of myself, and the ways I dealt with the world. I didn't like what I saw. I began to encourage her to be more aggressive, to stand up for her rights; like me, she seemed to accept too much. I was growing far too passive, falling into a somnambulent routine of staying in the house, cleaning it, doing the laundry, preparing the meals, taking care of Kathleen. If I wanted the car, I'd have to follow an intricate routine: I'd have to get up earlier, feed and dress Kathleen, drive John to school, return home. Then reverse the procedure: wake her from her nap in the afternoon or from her sleep if John worked late and drive to school to bring him home.

Now that I was not working or going to school, there was no excuse for having the laundry done outside, so I did it all, and all the ironing. With money so tight, I made all of Kathleen's clothes and had to be careful about shopping and planning meals; I became compulsive about keeping the house clean, trying to be model wife and mother—at least what I thought a model wife and mother should be.

I had always hated cleaning floors, but I really got into floor-waxing that year: I'd wax them incessantly. The porcelain in my bathrooms was always shiny. I became very resentful of the messes other people made—the tracks of the troops of kids that always came to our house because the other mothers wouldn't let them in, the residue of fingerpaints and Crayolas, the clothes and books and papers John left scattered about the house. Managing to set out an interesting dinner every night became my supreme accomplishment.

I felt silly complaining about such trivia to anybody, so I didn't.

Increasingly I became lonelier and lonelier. John was gone all the time now; he was very much burdened by his work, where he constantly locked horns with other administrators—ex-coaches who resented and felt threatened by a genuine educator—and by the fact that there was never time to work on his dissertation. He had to be the disciplinarian for the school, and all he did was pound little boys' fannies all day long. The principal measured his effectiveness by how often his name appeared in the graffiti in the boys' restrooms.

I could see his joy, optimism, self-confidence being ground away. He seldom laughed anymore—not the way he used to. He began to put on weight. Little was left of him but a heavy sense of responsibility—to his job, to finish the interminable dissertation, but most of all to us. When he came home at seven or eight or later in the evening, he was lost to me. I'd keep his dinner hot for him; he'd eat it in silence while he read the paper or watched TV, and then he'd flake out.

Graduate school had been temporary—and exciting. San Antonio was static—and it gave every hint of being what life would be for us from then on.

Sometimes we'd play bridge with John's boss and wife, or they'd come to our house; but I didn't like the people he worked with, and neither did he. We had few real friends now and our only "nights out" were to the San Antonio Symphony performances, which I enjoyed immensely; but they were too infrequent.

Now that we were in San Antonio, there were fewer

holiday trips; half the family was there, and more of it would arrive to pack the Sullivans' big house for the ritual occasions that existed to convince us that we were a family.

Such as Thanksgiving.

I'd always liked the large family gatherings—liked to be part of them, to hear the old stories and be part of the elaborate preparations. Only this year it was different.

Something strange was beginning to happen to me. I was beginning to close up, turn off. I would find myself crying, without warning, for no reason. At first I'd tell myself it was because I missed Glenda or my mother, who with my stepfather had just been transferred to Pakistan, and was unhappy there. But I knew they were just excuses. Something was deeply wrong—something I couldn't find, couldn't name. I cried; I left the house less; I didn't answer the phone.

I didn't want to go to the Sullivans' big house that year. I had never minded the Thanksgiving preparations and looked forward to seeing all the people, but this time, somehow, I began to see it in a different perspective.

When we got to the house, I went immediately to the kitchen and asked what was required of me. "Oh, honey, would you make a pan of cornbread and some biscuits, so we'll have that ready for the dressing? And if you don't want to make the biscuits, we can use the canned ones, but they aren't as good."

Okay.

Later, there were several trips to the store for extra butter, another half-gallon of milk, the whipping cream for one of the pies that was already in the refrigerator anyway but which nobody could find amid the stacks of casseroles, salads, and miscellaneous foil-wrapped packages. The turkey, a twenty-pounder, had been in the oven since dawn.

The extra leaves for the table had to be gotten out of the front closet, dusted, and set in place. Then the heavy padding that protected that table was laid on, and the damask cloth on top of that. Ellen and I worked as a team, smoothing it down, counting everybody once again, placing the silver and the napkins, and a crystal glass for everyone. *I don't think I want to be doing all this, I thought. Not this time. Not now.*

There were still flowers in the garden, and those went on the table, too, after they had been picked and arranged. In the den, the men talked about the football that season, and the staggering succession of games to be watched that day. The women were all in the kitchen, all of us trying to be useful, producing the staggering succession of dishes required by this feast. I wondered if I'd see a football game this year. It wasn't that I cared that much about football, but clearly they were having more fun in the den than we were in the kitchen.

We were being useful. Being useful in someone else's kitchen is a complex social ritual. I knew where everything was to be found, how each dish was to be prepared, but I kept getting into everybody else's way. I wanted to be elsewhere. Perhaps the other women wanted the same thing, too, but we never talked about it.

*What will happen if I take off my apron and do just that?* My share of the work would have fallen on Ellen; I would have violated the ritual. I couldn't do it. Heresy.

Getting everything on the table, hot, was sheer choreography. Turkey and dressing, candied yams, creamed onions, fresh green beans, scalloped oysters, cranberry sauce, glazed carrots, green salads and fruit salads, giblet gravy, pickles, and olives, and relishes of every imaginable kind. Homemade rolls (Aunt Nell's incomparable recipe) and homemade light bread. And there had to be room for dessert, because there were several kinds of pies, at least two cakes, and homemade peach ice cream from the freezer. Then coffee, and all the homemade candy that the visitors had brought, because that is the logical food that travels.

And always the ritualistic grace note: something was forgotten in the kitchen, and only remembered—with a flutter of embarrassment—when dessert was over. Broccoli with the cheese sauce and almonds, left somewhere in the disarray of the kitchen. Everyone would have laughed harder, if they could. But another part of the ritual was to eat oneself into a stupor.

Much groaning and patting of stomachs, many compliments for the old dishes that had been prepared just the same way as always—why, it wouldn't even *be* Thanksgiving dinner without them (the scalloped oysters exactly the way they were prepared ten-twenty-however-many years ago), while the new dishes rung in to make the meal exciting elicited appreciation as well—all to please the men.

When the men, stuffed to the point they declared they couldn't possibly look at food for a week, rose from the table, the elaborate exodus began. The men returned to the den and the football games on television. The women were left with the wreckage.

Wall-to-wall dirty dishes.

My mother-in-law was worn to a frazzle, and the prospect of the kitchen, with every vessel, pot, and pan dirty, with the dining-room table still laden with food and dirty dishes, seemed too much for her. All the days of preparation, all the work and planning, had led to this moment of exhaustion.

I begged her to go to bed, to take a nap. We'd clean everything up.

"Oh, I couldn't do that," she said. The duty, the obligations were not over.

"Please," I insisted.

"But I have to put the food away at least."

"No, we'll manage it all. You just try to get some rest."

Ellen and I looked at each other, shrugged our shoulders and set to work. Mama went to bed, feeling guilty.

*It's not fair. It's not fair to any of us,* I thought, turning to face the mountains of dishes, the food to be wrapped and saved, the floor that had to be mopped, the hours of deadwork before I could get back to my little house and find something of myself again.

The ivy kept burning up, the housework was never done, the women kept coming around with their incredible stories. I was horrified—and fascinated—to learn that several people on the block were having affairs. Sometimes during the day, sometimes at night; sometimes the spouses knew, sometimes they didn't. Somehow I got to know everthing. I became a repository for all these murky secrets, which they'd tell me and nobody else. I couldn't understand, and I was deeply troubled when Jean told me she was getting tangled up with her next-door neighbor.

Why would she want to do that? Why would *he?* Well, his wife had told me she was frigid. I was privy to all sorts of such intimate, sordid news. I didn't want to get involved in it; I didn't ever want that to happen to me.

But I couldn't stop the continuing narrative. "Gee," one of them would say when a new family moved into the neighborhood, "that Al is really a sexy guy!" Then the next installment, in a week or so: "Well, we had dinner with Al and Susie, and everybody got a little smashed. Al kissed me in the kitchen. Wow!" And then, to my horror and embarrassment, since I knew everyone involved, the details would become explicit. And the story would go on, week after week, building with all sorts of complications and revelations, interspersed with visions from the religious fanatic down the street, the ramblings from the woman who drank too much, the stories from the woman whose husband only wanted sex, and Kathleen saying, "Mama, Mama, Mama, look. Look, Mama, look. No, Mama . . . turn your *face* around and look. You can't see that way. Look, Mama!"

Why did they tell *me* all their stories? Perhaps because I didn't disapprove—overtly? Perhaps I got some kind of vicarious pleasure out of listening to them. After all, they were at least making mischief; I wasn't doing anything at all. I could see then that a lot of it came from boredom, a search for excitement that we all missed; they had no other excitement in their lives, no passion.

The frightening thing was that they were like me.

They were trapped and bored. Bored. Bored. Bored. Perhaps they were somewhat less well-educated than I was, and rather envious about that, but what difference did it make? I couldn't see that my education was doing me any good. I, too, was trapped and I was bored. My neighbors were only a little farther along. But how long would it be before I caught up?

They could complain, let some of it out; I couldn't. They were out of whack but somehow coping. I didn't want to be like them. Not ever. I tried to hold everything in.

And I tried to fight it. I made a point of meeting some new people at church, whom we more or less liked and saw occasionally. It became an awful effort—as it never had been before—to do that kind of thing. We both liked the Episcopal priest and his wife, and spent as much time with them as we could. That helped—for a while. But most of our social life consisted of command performances with people with whom we had little in common—cookouts or hunting trips with the principal of John's school and some of the other ex-coach administrators. We had few people in for dinner because we couldn't afford it—except John's parents, who brought their own.

I made some attempts to find work, and had several long discussions with the man at the San Antonio *Express* who did all the cultural criticism—art, music, drama, and dance. I tried to talk him into letting me take over the art criticism, which he was admittedly not well-qualified to do. I knew the art scene in San Antonio well—the galleries and the artists—and I could have taken Kathleen along with me to shows. But the *Express* was not hiring. I went to both museums in town and both were anxious to put me to work, but only as a volunteer; they had no funds for additional staff. I wanted to do it, but there was no way we could afford to have me work for nothing.

I looked desperately for something to do, anything to keep the bottom from falling out of my life. I couldn't even help John on his dissertation as long as he wasn't doing any work on it himself.

The most superficial concerns became paramount to me. Cleaning the house. Planning the meals. Waxing those stupid floors. Scrubbing the tile in the shower. Ironing John's white shirts. Seeing that Kathleen had plenty to do. At night, those single-minded concerns were what I'd talk to John about; that's all I thought about, and all I had to discuss.

I did less and less reading. I wrote fewer and fewer letters to my family, to Glenda. I fiendishly cleaned the house. I tried harder and harder to be Supermom, reading to Kathleen, making things with her, encouraging all sorts of creative activities, having all the kids on the block in to draw pictures, paint, have tea parties, and play dress-up— no matter what the mess, how many pieces of puzzles and toys had to be found and sorted, how much paint had to be washed up how often. I geared my life completely to Kathleen's. I got up when she got up and ate when she was hungry; I napped when she napped. All my bodily functions were attuned to those of other people—to John, to Kathleen. There was no guarantee I could finish a letter to Glenda uninterrupted, or even go to the bathroom by myself.

"Mama, Mama. Look. No, Mama. Turn around and look, Mama." I listened and I looked. I tried very hard to pay good attention. I spent hours appliquéing and embroidering fanciful birds, made out of scraps from my old maternity smocks, on her bedroom curtain. Then I felt guilty about not spending the time with her instead.

I began to cry more, and felt guilty about my crying, and tried to hide it from John and Kathleen.

I began to feel a tightness in my throat, a choking feeling.

Something really desperate was happening to me. I began to sleep fully as much as Kathleen did and to want more. I could feel a slow gearing-down and closing-up process working in me, as if the compartments in my head were locking shut, one by one, door by door.

I became frantic. I had quit thinking. I had lost everything. I remembered how once, for two whole months, I'd been wildly excited about Frederick II of Sicily—his Italian city-state problems and his confrontations with the popes. I had no concerns like that anymore, could hardly believe that I ever had had. Frederick II! Art history! Life had ground down to a halt. I had no center left. I was living under water.

I gave up *Foreign Affairs* for my neighbors' affairs.

I rarely left the house, and had come to the point where I didn't want anyone coming inside. My life would never change. It would always be the same; we'd always live in that tacky little house with never enough money to make ends meet, with all those troops of children underfoot, with all those worn, hysterical, trapped women telling me unbelievable stories I didn't want to hear. It was all too big; it was mashing me into its particular mold and style. I couldn't fight it, I didn't know how to fight: someone had stolen all my tools.

I knew what was going to happen the next day, and the next day, and the next, forever and ever, amen.

I hated it all but could find no valid reason for my hatred. What I did every day was what the magazines I read devoted hundreds of pages to celebrating and explicating every month. We were everything Young Marrieds should be. It took two to sustain a family; John had prepared himself to make a living, and my job was to stay put and make a home. Our jobs were clearly distributed out of economic necessity.

Nothing was working out the way any of us had been told we could expect it to. Something was very much amiss, something deeper than the problems we could all name. Those kinds of troubles were thoroughly discussed in the women's magazines we all bought and read. They weren't problems, they were symptoms.

I kept trying desperately to learn the trade of housewife/mother better. My magazines told me these were the most deeply satisfying things a woman could do. Maybe if

I did everything *better* it would all begin to fall into place, I could stop being so weird. I had once imagined myself having a house, keeping it, raising a child; I had not imagined the details. Nor how constant they would be. I was putting all my energy into something I had always taken for granted, that John still took for granted; it was giving me nothing in return.

As I think back on that year, I realize how much of it I've blotted out. There is that sameness about it all—one day running into the next; days so much the same I can't differentiate them. I know now it was a kind of existence so essentially abnormal it was bound to produce some kind of craziness. Only its familiarity prevented me from seeing, then, just how crazy-making it was. But at that time I could see no reason why I was crying, constantly, why I began to have that repeated fantasy, stronger and stronger, that I was dead.

Yes, I was dead. *Why doesn't anyone notice?*

I became meticulous about my appearance. Because I went out, anywhere, so seldom, going out became an event of the first magnitude and dressing impeccably a compulsion. I added a fashion magazine to my regular magazine intake and read it religiously every month. I saved pennies to go to Frost Brothers, the fanciest department store in San Antonio, to have my hair cut. It cost twelve dollars, a lot of pennies, and I'd have to listen to the hairdresser talk about his latest trip to Acapulco. Then I had to leave him a tip. My perfect façade was absolutely necessary to hide the mess underneath. It protected that mess—me—from the world, and it was pretty fragile.

Money. Why wasn't there more of it? Just a little for myself that I could spend any way I chose. If I had it, I could do all those things I wanted to do. I could fix up our little house; it could have been pretty. I'd be able to hire a sitter once in a while and get away from that bare street with its scraggly trees and all those children and women. John and I could go out—to dinner. Oh God, how wonderful it would be, just to go *out* to dinner! Money meant mobility—and some relief from the boredom. I wished for better clothes, for all of us.

Instead, I sewed; and I became compulsive about every seam and button. I'd sew little straps in the inside of my sleeveless dresses, so I could snap in my bra and slip straps. *They must not show.*

That was really nuts. Visible underwear straps became a big horror. Avoiding them was just part of the effort to build an impenetrable and perfect façade to hide behind until I got well.

I still looked forward to going to church. But it meant all the hazards of getting out, seeing some people. I kept thinking it was important that Kathleen go to church, though she was never too impressed with the whole business. In the Episcopal church they have a childrens' Sunday school at the same time as the regular church services; the children participate in a service of their own. I asked Kathleen about it one time, about what they did. "Oh," she said, "we stand-ed up and kneel-ed down, just like in the big church. Big deal."

I have a photograph of Kathleen taken at that time, and it tears my heart to look at it, though today she says she only remembers it all as a happy time. In the photograph she is sitting on the couch, clutching a pillow, with her funny little skinny pigtails, and her ironed T-shirt. An *ironed* T-shirt. She looks far too solemn for a four-year-old with her big starey eyes.

I tried not to cry in front of her, but children that age

see everything. I'd be doing the dishes and tears would start to flow. "What's wrong, Mama?" she'd say. "What's wrong, Mama? Mama?" and I'd have to turn away from my baby and try to dry my eyes before answering her.

I was going crazy. I knew it. And I'd do permanent damage to my child in the process.

I was afraid to go out because I couldn't depend on myself not to burst into tears. I kept it hidden from John for a long time, which wasn't hard since he was gone so much. But I became weepier and weepier. And I felt guilty because I could see nothing to cry about. With what the other women told me, it was clear that I was much better off than they; yet in spite of their problems, they were at least able to adjust to them and find ways to entertain themselves. None of them were falling apart like I was, I thought. What valid reason did I have for being unhappy, downright crazy?

My mother, in Pakistan, noticed that my letters often sounded depressed. She began to write me at great length all the reasons why I should be happy: I had a nice house, a lovely daughter, a loving husband who would never look at another woman; I had a good education, I had my health, what more could I want? Every mother alive had gone through what I was experiencing. They'd survived. She herself, she told me, had had an awfully bad time when my brother and I were small and Pappy was away so much. She often felt like she was losing her marbles, but she had survived. The women around me were surviving. Was that all there was to it, all I could hope for—just to *survive*? Was there some impatience in my genes that other women didn't have?

*Why? Why?* There was no reason.

So I cried, and felt tired all the time—a supreme fatigue—it was all I could do just to get out of bed in the morning and drag myself from chore to chore. My concentration was zilch.

Along with the choking feeling, the tightness in my throat, my hands began to shake. A slow tremor worked its way through my body, through my hands. Holding a tea cup, I'd suddenly hear it begin to rattle.

My life wasn't that physically exhausting. Get up. Feed and dress Kathleen, straighten the house, do the laundry, fix lunch, do the dishes while Kathleen napped, have some of her friends in for tea parties or games, start dinner. It was a fairly leisurely routine.

But it was all endless, forever.

I couldn't see an end to Kathleen's demands on me, because they were still constant after four years. I could not envison a time when I would not be tied to that little house, to everyone's needs but my own. I had no control over my life. John noticed nothing until I started crying all the time, uncontrollably, day and night.

I began to put my hand over my mouth.

Why? Because I was afraid of what I might say? To hold it all in? But I couldn't keep it locked in any longer.

"What's the matter, honey?" he asked. "What on earth is the matter, why are you crying? Why do you put your hand over your mouth all the time like that?"

I had no idea, I told him. I could no more articulate it to him than I could to myself.

"What can I do for you to make it better?"

I didn't know. I didn't know what was wrong.

"Can't I do *anything* to help?"

"You're doing everything you can," I told him quietly, tears running down my cheeks, my throat growing dry and tight. "You're *trying*, John. You're being so sweet. I just . . . I just can't say what's wrong with me . . . nothing *could* be wrong with me . . ."

Something terrible was happening to me that I couldn't share with him. Not at all.

My mother-in-law and my mother—all the way from Pakistan—kept asking the same questions: "What's wrong? What's wrong?" They repeated the familiar litany: I had a nice home, a wonderful daughter, a loving husband. I was young, intelligent. "You have *everything*, Judy. What's wrong? What could *possibly* be wrong?"

"I don't know. I don't know," I said, choking.

There was magic in my church to help me. Some priests, though it was something of an embarrassment and generally frowned upon, held healing services. I checked around and found one such parish and went one Wednesday morning. It was an old church, in a strange part of town. A motley clutch of people, most of them old and sick, were kneeling, praying in the front of the nave. Kathleen and I silently joined them, and I prayed first that nobody had anything she might catch. There was a Communion service, then we all went back to the altar rail and knelt again as the priest passed from one to another, gently laying his hands on our bowed heads, murmuring the prayer for the sick.

My poor sick head. It needed some good magic. Maybe this would fix it.

Well, it didn't.

John became terribly upset. He thought the problem might be helped by seeing a doctor, and took me to a general practitioner who listened with patience and puzzlement.

"Many young mothers seem to be having your problem," he said, and gave me a prescription for tranquilizers.

I took them, but they only made me catatonic. I felt just as miserable—but at a lower rate of speed. It was hard enough to get through my days as it was, I certainly didn't need a chemical handicap. And I hated the very idea of taking them; they gave me the willies. Being *frantic* with despair was more my style than being paralyzed with it. Taking drugs to protect yourself from feeling seemed indecent.

When I was miserable and crying at night, John would say: "Take some more of your pills." He was concerned, but he was also tired and out of patience. He knew that if I took the tranquilizers, at least I'd shut up.

*What I really need*, I thought, *is a frontal lobotomy*. That would have fixed me up fine—for myself, for the others.

The doctor hadn't been much help, so I went back to the church again; I began to see our priest. He asked what I was upset about and I told him I didn't know. He asked me what worried me, and what I did all day. I told him I wanted Kathleen to have the best upbringing possible.

"Do you throw her out into the street?"

"No," I said. "I entertain her, we have tea parties, I read to her, we play dress-up."

"Then that shouldn't worry you."

He was reasonable and patient; he tried to be very supportive. Was he being patronizing? I was too far gone for the there-there-my-dear-everything's-going-to-be-just-fine routine. I knew it and he knew it.

"Be happy in your work," I'd say to myself as I swept the floors and scrubbed the toilets. "Be happy in your work." That's what the commandant of the prison camp in *The Bridge on the River Kwai* said to his British officer-gentlemen prisoners who were made to dig latrines. I felt like a prisoner of war who had missed the war, in a prison camp I had not been prepared for. I envied men in the Army, trained to sustain themselves through periods of severe limitation. I had never been given such mental discipline.

And every day continued to be so much like the day that preceded it and the day that would follow. It was all so permanent. And I cried, and felt that dreadful choking in my throat, and kept checking to see if my underwear straps were showing, and tried to lay low and be unseen, and Kathleen said, "Mama, Mama," and I wanted to *be* there with her, really *there,* and do everything I was supposed to do, that was expected of me, the right way, the way it should be done, perfectly, but there was that awful deep-down clutching feeling, always, and the tears that never stopped and my hand always going to my mouth— to hold back what? It was all so damned permanent.

If John told me it wouldn't last, that this stage of our life would some day be over, his words made no impression on me. I had shrunk to almost nothing. I *was* nothing. Nobody. I could only assimilate what was immediately, concretely useful. Anything positive, encouraging, anyone said to me just became one more damned good reason for feeling guiltier than ever.

The Mexican psychiatrist at the clinic was hand-picked for me by our priest. He was a pleasant old man in his seventies, and had no more idea what was wrong with me than anyone else.

The out-patient clinic of the state hospital had a rule— in order to be treated you had to commit yourself to the hospital. I remember laughing wildly: here I was supposed to be absolutely out of my tree and I was signing my own commitment papers. It was the first thing that had struck me as funny in months.

When I wrote to my mother in Pakistan that I was seeing a psychiatrist, it distressed her awfully. Like me, she must have been convinced that a mother is endlessly responsible (and endlessly guilty) for every psychological problem her child might have. "Oh, baby," she wrote, "where did I fail you? What did I do wrong?"

I read the letter with despair. Couldn't I do anything right? Couldn't I even go crazy without someone else feeling she had to take the blame?

Dr. Sanchez said I was doing exactly what I was supposed to be doing; I just wasn't doing it well. My attitude was wrong: if I were a *real* woman, I'd be fulfilled by my life.

I think he took me on to entertain himself. I tried hard enough to oblige. Most of the patients were working-class Mexican-Americans, and I was at least out of the pattern—except that most of his other patients were women, too. "Tell me about yourself," he said at our first session, and I answered, "Well, I'm a housewife," because that's the only way I saw myself. We never quite had a meeting of minds; I'm only thankful that he wasn't a Freudian—he vehemently declared right in the beginning that he had no use for any of those "clever Jewish intellectuals"—I'd probably still be committed.

He was a small plump man with a lot of heavy curly white hair, and if he'd had a beard he'd have looked like Santa Claus. He was very kindly, very gentle, and very sloppy. Ashes from his cigar blew up and scattered so often over all his clothes he was a fire hazard. He had a slight Spanish accent, he loved to make literary allusions—

"Do you feel like Madame Bovary?"—and he often talked about chamber music, an interest we had in common.

I hated to go there. It meant that I had to go *out*. I made special arrangements for Kathleen to stay at a nursery school for just a few hours, and I also had to arrange to keep the car. I had to drive by myself (which Dr. Sanchez and John insisted I do) through heavy city traffic for an hour, then sit in that nightmarish waiting room with all the blank looks and twitches. All the way over, all the time I waited, I'd think of what I wanted to talk about. I wanted to be through as soon as possible, and I made myself promise I'd never lie to him, that I'd be perfectly straight; sometimes I'd make a statement, then say, "No, I'm coloring that to make myself look better."

More than that, though, I was determined not to bore the man to death. He'd rock back and forth in his swivel chair, turn and look out the window, scatter some cigar ashes, and thumb idly through an art book he always kept on a bookstand beside his desk. Which infuriated me. I was pleased with myself when I genuinely amused or interested him, frantic when I could tell he was bored. He had respect for my intelligence and my abilities, and that's what I hadn't had—someone to say, "Yes, you're a valuable, interesting human being." To John and Kathleen, who both loved me deeply but who related to me chiefly in terms of their needs, I'm afraid I was just a household appliance.

Dr. Sanchez kept a large box of Kleenex on his desk, and would lean over now and then to hand me a tissue. I cried a lot at first, decimating on the average a quarter of a box per visit. "How do you feel about John?" he asked one day. When I effusively told him how much I loved and respected John, how grateful I was to him for his kindness, he implied that I was protesting too much, that I must be unhappy in my marriage. How was our sex life?

I was not prepared to deal with a question like that. Nor was he prepared to understand what it was like for me to have so little time for myself or control over my life that I couldn't even count on going to the bathroom alone. My very life belonged to other people—chiefly, my child. He wasn't interested in talking about that. He allowed as how he'd never been able to spend much time with his ten children when they were small. What a pity, he said. How wonderful, how challenging it must be to watch a little mind, a little body grow and develop! Why hadn't he spent more time with *his* children? They got on his nerves, interrupted his train of thought so often. Never mind about that, he really wanted to know about my sex life. I didn't find *that* relevant. I thought my sex life was okay, and anyway, how can you discuss something like that with so little basis for comparison—like none? So both those fertile fields went ineffectively explored. He discussed child rearing strictly theoretically while I complained from practice; he questioned my sexual practices and I replied with theories I'd read about.

I did talk a lot about some of the frustrations I felt, how I disliked being a person to whom things happen rather than a person who does things.

But why didn't I find being with Kathleen, as she grew and developed, thrilling and exciting? *That* was doing something. We were back to his children again, and his even more numerous grandchildren. His practice kept him so busy. And there was the problem of their getting on his nerves, so much worse now that he was older and less patient.

For a while, during the Cuban missile crisis, I began to

come alive again. I was scared. The crisis was very real to us in San Antonio and we kept the car ready at all times, full of gas, packed with supplies and foodstuffs. Lake Travis, where John's father kept a houseboat, was sparsely populated; we could head for the hills, live on the houseboat, be safe there.

I couldn't help welcoming the crisis: it was *something to do.*

"You're a very intelligent person," Dr. Sanchez told me. "You're very fortunate to have an education, and you should be able because of your intelligence to plan your life better, so you can do more efficiently those things that frustrate you—and then have time to do the things you really want to do."

"But I *can't* do them properly," I argued—not saying, "I don't *want* to," or there was just too much to do that amounted to too little.

"The trouble, I think," Dr. Sanchez said one afternoon, turning from the window to face me, "is simply that you are spoiled, willful, and rebellious."

I looked at him for a long moment without saying a word. Was it so? Was that *really* it? I'd been willful and rebellious in refusing my debut. Mama had said so.

All right, if that's what I was, then how could I live with it, I asked him. How could I change?

"You're a valuable person," he said.

But I found that hard to believe. No one else was telling me that.

"It's a shame not to make use of your gifts, not to use them to best advantage."

More guilt.

I had enough guilt. If he thought I was so special, what was I supposed to do about that? In every way he could,

Dr. Sanchez was giving me the same message I had gotten from everybody else all my life. That message was that I should happily give myself up, heart and soul, all of me, for my husband and my family. John's mother did it: teaching all day and then coming home at night and knocking herself out being the best possible wife and mother, to make up for being gone all day. My mother had done it, all of her life given over to other people. Was I so different from other women, wanting something more than that? Did I have to feel guilty for not wanting to be a martyr? They didn't see their lives in those terms, why should I?

*Spoiled, willful, and rebellious.* Was that really what I was? *Valuable but rebellious. Will-less, willful.*

At least Dr. Sanchez listened to me. I had been listening to everyone else for so long.

At least he saw, or came to see, the guilt—to know that it was the root of my paralysis. During the last days, when I was crying less and liking myself more, he told me: "You have felt so guilty for so long, and for so little, that you ought to have a license to sin for the rest of your life."

Somehow, for all the confusion and all the misunderstanding, I came to feel in the three months that I saw him that perhaps I *was* in some way special. I began to see that my "weirdness" *was* a positive attribute, and that just by exercising more self-discipline I'd be able to do all those things I was worried about out of proportion, plus those other activities I wanted to do and considered more worthwhile.

Maybe it was having someone listen to *me* for a change—even though, at times, it was like conversing with a Martian. Instead of just *giving* attention myself all the time I could *take* a little comfort, a little solace, a little attention for *me;* I'd been passing out those things continually. Maybe the only way I could have gotten them *was* to go crazy.

I had used up innumerable boxes of Kleenex in Dr. Sanchez's office, but at the end I wasn't crying anymore. And I wasn't dead anymore. It took three months to dam up the flow.

It took seven more years for me to be able to see exactly what was wrong with the job he'd done on my head putting me back together, and why the glue wouldn't hold forever.

# Three

## The Dress
## and
## Girdle Life

# 9

## Delicious Solitude

One morning, a year later, I woke up early to the ringing of an alarm clock. I hadn't needed one in years—Kathleen always woke me.

I felt instinctively across the bed for John, but it was a new bed—John was not there.

I was alone, in a different house. I sat up, yawned with luxuriant slowness, smiled, and looked over at the alarm clock: I wouldn't have to make breakfast for John or Kathleen, wouldn't have to feed or dress, or worry about anyone but myself, so I still had plenty of time. There was absolutely no need to hurry.

My clothes were folded neatly on the chair, where I'd left them the night before. The room was spotless: I wouldn't have to clean a thing. I might not even make the bed. I peeked down at the floor: John's clothes weren't there.

It was no dream. I was alone, and I had absolutely nothing to do but get up, dress myself, trot off to classes, and then spend the whole day exactly, precisely, the way

*I* wanted to spend it. I might read for a few hours or I might not; I might call up an old friend, but I probably wouldn't; in the evening I'd no doubt take out my cello and play for myself.

With an enormous sigh—so joyous I felt immoral about it—I put my arms out at right angles to my side and, like a sky-diver, keeled straight backward onto the pillow.

It was summer, and I was in Denton by myself, without John or Kathleen; all I had to do was take several courses in my master's program. For six weeks. Six *whole* weeks. I had not one other responsibility—not to anyone.

The year since I'd last seen Dr. Sanchez had been an exceptionally good one for me. John had accepted a teaching job at Emporia State Teachers College; the pay was lower than he was getting as a vice-principal, but teaching would give him time to finish his dissertation, and they had promised him a "substantial" raise when it was completed. John was my whole life, and I wanted him to be happy. I knew he hadn't been happy in San Antonio, and it hadn't exactly been a picnic for me either, so at the end of only one year we sold our little house there and escaped to Emporia, Kansas.

It felt like escape to me. I was relieved to be leaving San Antonio and all the problems it had meant, but I felt, too, that I was just running away from a lot of those problems, not really dealing with them.

All I could remember about Kansas, from having driven through it once when I was a child, was flat, bare-assed prairie; but Emporia turned out to be a very lovely college town. Two rivers meet there and the town is filled with large elm trees and many old wood-frame and brick houses. Kathleen immediately made good friends with a neighbor's daughter and we registered her for kindergarten in the college laboratory school, which had been one of John's stipulations; it was excellent.

When Kathleen started school I did something I'd always wanted to do: I began studying cello at the college. I'd taken piano lessons for many years as a child, Mama's idea, and I could play the ukelele, she had taught me, but the cello was what I'd always wanted to learn.

*Violoncello.*

I loved the very sound of its name, I loved the way it looked, I loved the way it sounded. I practiced like a maniac. The curious thing is that I really wasn't any good at it and I didn't care; I loved it anyway. It was the first thing I'd done that I wanted to do, and it wasn't somebody else's idea.

My cello teacher, a Bostonian, was a big, lovely bear of a man who couldn't understand my Texas accent. That made us even: I couldn't understand him either. During lessons in his studio on the third floor of the college music building, he'd say something I couldn't understand, I'd reply unintelligibly, and he'd blow a fuse. He'd yell: "I don't see how Kennedy and Johnson run this country! They must send each other memos! They can never have any conversations. *We* certainly can't!"

We'd walk downstairs together with our big cases—both of us afraid that I, with my bad eyes and general clumsiness, would fall on my instrument or, worse, on his—and then out we'd step into a brisk Kansas wind. My cello, light as a feather but almost as big as I was, would catch the wind like a kite, and I'd wrestle it in the general direction of the parking lot. What I needed, I thought, was a skateboard. With the cello for a sail, who'd need a car?

John was glad to be back in the classroom, excited about the innovative programs at the college; his old optimism seemed to be back again.

Good touring programs came through Emporia to the college regularly, and we saw all the plays, went to poetry readings and lectures, heard every string quartet and orchestra concert. Or at least, Kathleen and I did—John often worked evenings on the dissertation. We played a lot of bridge with members of his department, and at John's AAUP meetings made friends with people from other departments whom I came to like very much. Kathleen was happy with school, John was more content than I'd seen him in ages; and with the outside chance of someday teaching a course or two for the art department, I went back to Denton to work further on my master's, which took three more summers to complete.

I went alone, without John or Kathleen. I had moved from my father's house into my husband's, with a year of college in between; this would be the first time I'd ever lived alone in my life.

When several of my new friends remarked that it was peculiar, me going off like that, I explained that it was a tradition in John's family: his mother had done the same thing to finish her master's. His family had always put a high premium on education; sacrifices were to be made to go to school.

Besides, it wasn't as if I was leaving the family to fend for itself. Kathleen would be happy visiting with relatives, just as I had on those marvelous summer visits when I was young. It was fun to live in a communal family—moving from household to household all summer long, like delighted gypsies. Kathleen was as excited about the prospect as I'd always been at her age.

John liked his comforts but he wasn't selfish; he knew that I'd be happy back at college, and he kept encouraging me to finish my degree. Neither of us had a wandering eye, so there were no worries there, and John was proud enough of his own cooking to enjoy making his own meals.

So off Kathleen went to visit her grandparents in Texas, as John as well as I had always done, and I headed down to Denton.

Something inside me began to bloom that summer.

A couple of artists rented me their house very cheaply, in exchange for my watering the yard and the plants. It was very much an artist's house—decorated with taste and a loving eye for visual detail. Surrounded by shade trees, the house stayed cool except during the hottest part of the day. It was an old house, so the ceilings were high and the rooms large. Everything—the paintings, the furniture, the walls—was a blend of pastel blues and grays and greens. A family of cardinals fed at the feeder on the windowsill while I ate my breakfast every morning. I would sit for long hours in one of the handmade pieces of furniture, looking at the paintings; it was an *artist's* house, a house that made me feel at home. I remember seeing the grass and the plants through the hot Denton summer.

What I remember most was the utterly delicious sensation of being completely alone.

I was responsible for no one but myself.

Miracle of miracles, that spacious and gentle house never got messed up.

There were no dirty dishes to pick up.

There was never anyone in the bathroom when I wanted it.

I could scarcely find a whole washerload of laundry to do in a week.

I never had to cook—and there were no dirty dishes to speak of.

And in the evenings, as I sat by myself reading or playing my cello, it was quiet and still and luxuriantly peaceful.

Yes, something inside me began to bloom that summer. I studied as long as I wanted; I worked for hours into the middle of the day or night: I set my own pace every day. I began to discover new things that I could do—and the most important discovery was that I could be by myself and not die of loneliness, that I, Judy, existed whole and separate from others.

The course work in art history, which by now was my defined major, was fairly interesting, though I soon felt—and knew—I wasn't being pushed enough. I was beginning to set my own standards, and they were higher than what I found around me. I'd have liked to study with Sherman Lee, a scholar in Cleveland whom I'd read and much admired. I'd have liked to go some place with a better academic reputation, somewhere that would be a real challenge—where I could play marbles with the big boys.

For the first time I began to regret, consciously, that none of that was possible. I was married. I was a wife. I was a mother.

I felt a tension inside me, pushing me toward my own private desires, pulling me away from my family—a steady tugging that gave me occasional twinges of guilt: for I wanted to do those things I had chosen already not to do, roads removed from what I was supposed to do.

I had to take studio as well as history courses on my degree, and one class I chose was metalwork. I found I had a talent for stake raising: taking a flat sheet of metal, annealing it with fire and acid until it's soft, then shaping it with a hammer against a steel stake, into a hollow form. I had an easy facility for the process that everybody else in the class found difficult to impossible. For me, it was a delight. I could pound out my frustrations and would work happily away at it for hours. Like playing my cello. But like that, too, there was a small problem with the finished product. The things I worked so hard to make were never as beautiful as I envisioned they would be. Usually, they ended up looking like an artifact from the early Bronze Age.

Sometimes walking to class or to the library, I'd suddenly think: *I really ought to be missing John and Kathleen more than I do.* But I wasn't—not at all. I'd think: *If I'd ever lived this way before, I'd probably never have chosen another way.*

To have that much privacy—of person and purposes—was wonderful. I couldn't get over it. I luxuriated in my bounty.

Now and again I'd have a friend from school come over to the house, and we'd fix a simple dinner; but most of the time I preferred to be alone. One woman friend was also away from her children, and when I asked if she missed them she said, equivocating, that she did and she didn't.

I felt much the same way, I realized, after John and Kathleen came to stay with me for a few days. I loved seeing them, but frankly was not sorry to see them leave. I loved that house—so clean and neat—and within hours after John arrived, he'd pulled the mattress off the bed and into the living room, where the one air-conditioner was, left a trail of clothes and dishes all about. Kathleen's toys and clothes were scattered from hell to breakfast. All of a sudden the whole place was destroyed.

A few days before I had to return to Emporia, I was

walking alone toward the college, where I was going to meet some friends and drive out to the lake for a swim. I remember seeing a very young woman on the second-story porch of an old wood-frame house. There was a baby on the porch, in a playpen, and a toddler running around and making a lot of racket. The woman looked so lonely, so harried and bored, sitting up there on that hot day.

I had been bouncing down the street with my swimming satchel in my hand and some books to read as if I hadn't a care in the world.

She looked down at me just as I looked up at her. She watched me for several long moments, and I can remember thinking: *She really envies me.* I could almost feel it; she wished me in her place, and off to wherever I was off to. Just *off*, and free as I was.

But I wasn't free.

And I felt a strong urgency to tell her: "Look, I'm just on parole. It's not what you think it is. I have to go back—soon, soon."

John came with me to Denton the next summer, while Kathleen visited John's mother, and it was not the same.

He was finally finishing his dissertation, and I found myself ankle-locked at the typewriter for him again. I'd go to my classes until one, then head back and start typing.

But now I had work of my own, and after several weeks told him: "Look, I'll have to do my stuff first from now on."

He looked up at me from a book he was reading, but said nothing.

"I'll do all of your typing for you, but I've got to do my work while I'm fresh. I simply have to have my mind on it, John. It's important to me, and I can't do it after hours of this monkey work. Maybe it will slow me down, and I'll make more mistakes on yours when I'm tired, but I have got to do my work first. Can you understand?"

He said he did, and I continued the summer that way—but it was a summer without the tranquility I'd had the year before.

I was glad when it was over.

The teeny one-room apartment I had that third summer in Denton was so small it gave me cabin fever. No matter. I had a place to myself again.

Again I lived entirely according to my own schedule. I stayed up nights, writing my thesis. In the mornings I lay out in the sun and baked myself brown. I slept and ran and exercised. I could read for five hours about some ancient Japanese paintings undisturbed. I had no more classes to take and the research for my paper had all been completed the preceding winter.

I lived on hard-boiled eggs and sandwiches made of matzoh, cheese, and onion. Who was there to smell my breath?

I wore a bathing suit outside in the sun, in the apartment I wore nothing at all. Less laundry that way. In the mirror I ceased to recognize myself physically: I was lean, mahogany-colored, different. The cosmetics' clerk at the drugstore suggested that perhaps I had overdone it since I was buying a shade of make-up she usually sold only to "colored ladies." No matter. Days and days went by and I spoke to no one, wanted to speak with no one. Didn't need to.

*I really should spend some time with some of my old professors*, I'd think; but didn't. I ate when I wanted. I seldom went anywhere but to the grocery store. It was simply glorious.

"Everything's fine at home," John would assure me with our weekly phone call. The dinner invitations were still pouring in. Kathleen was having a marvelous time at camp that summer, was getting on beautifully.

I wondered, shocked at myself for even having the thought: *Is it possible they really don't* need *me?*

My mother died two years after we moved to Emporia. The Red Cross wired me that she was gravely ill, that she was being flown from Pakistan to a special hospital in Landstuhl, Germany, for an operation. Three days later, my brother and I were at her bedside.

When I first saw her in that hospital in the little town in the Saar Basin, I was struck immediately by how very much my mother had changed.

I was told she had a brain tumor. Mama was barely fifty.

Her head had been shaved—all her lovely hair was gone. As sick as she was, she always kept her head covered; no one must see her that way. The doctors planned to operate at once. Mama could barely speak, and when she did she could not always say what she meant. Words without meaning. Words with meanings opposite to what she meant.

The doctors made additional tests, then decided not to operate. Mama, they told us, had lung cancer as well as the brain tumor. There was cancer everywhere: she could not possibly live more than a few months.

I felt such rage that it should happen to her; she was so young, she and Papa had such a good life, they had been looking forward to a trip around the world when they returned from Pakistan—they had so many plans. While I was stunned, in a state of shock, Papa—a quiet pillar of strength for so many years—and my brother gave vent to their feelings a lot more directly.

Both of them absolutely went to pieces.

They had been so dependent on Mama, it was so painful to watch them, victims of the same tragedy—Papa the worst. Mama was going to die, but he was going to have to try to live without her. Worrying about that, and trying to comfort the two of them, trying to hide their distress from her, all of that kept my mind somewhat off my own pain and loss.

Papa arranged a transfer for himself to Fort Sam Houston in San Antonio so that Mama could be at Brooke Army Medical Center. I went home to Emporia to get Kathleen started in school, then returned to Texas.

Mama had responded well to the X-ray treatments and the chemical therapy; the doctors had been able to shrink her tumors, relieve some of the pain, and release her from the hospital. She could talk better, and looked infinitely better than she had in Germany. But we were told she had about four months to live. She was very weak and needed a great deal of care. Papa couldn't do it all. John's sister Ellen was in Emporia looking after my household; I felt very grateful for that, because it allowed me to have that time with Mama. She was dying and she knew it. But it was never discussed. She wanted me to stay and was uncharacteristically unconcerned about my being away from John and Kathleen. I wanted to make one more try at getting better acquainted with her.

I had always had the feeling that my mother, John, and a lot of other relatives and friends who loved me, saw me as something I wasn't.

Suddenly I wanted, quite desperately, to make a connection with my mother—on a frequency we'd never

130    *Mama Doesn't Live Here Anymore*

touched before. I wanted her to *know* me—what I was really like as a person, my deepest interests and ambitions. And I wanted her to do the same with me.

But there was a shadow between us.

We reminisced about Hamilton, about Japan, about all the places we'd lived, and I began to tell her small incidents from my private life. When I was sixteen, in Japan, I'd met a marvelous twenty-eight-year-old marine who could tango like Valentino; I'd brought him to the house for dinner. We had three or four dates, and then I refused to see or speak to him.

"He was really a charmer, and so handsome! Why, he used to bring us both roses every time he came to the house," Mama said.

"You never knew why I was so mean to him, did you?" I asked.

"You really were ugly," she said. "I remember fussing at you about it. You weren't rude very often."

I told her I'd found out he was married, and that this had horrified me. "Somehow," I said, trying to break through to my beautiful, sweet, funny mother, whom I had always wanted to be like, "I always had the idea that you had to be protected. I didn't want you to be upset or hurt."

We had developed fictions. I knew it now. A whole, intricate artificial structure that kept us apart even as it held us together. In recent years, in letters expert at making me feel guilty for not writing often enough to her and to other members of the family, she had maintained the fiction that the family still was close. But it wasn't. We all had very little in common. We were not what she imagined us to be. We were not the family she had had for so many years in the small, self-contained and comfortable world of

Hamilton. I did not know her; she did not know me. We were insulated from each other.

I tried to make her understand my interest in continuing school, wanting to teach; she couldn't fathom that kind of ambition and, as I thought of it, I couldn't understand it yet myself. Ambition was only beginning to define itself in me.

Mama was in bed most of the time, and I'd take care of her basic physical needs—bringing her food, polishing her nails, doing her shopping, entertaining her. I knew that when our talks grew serious she would get upset and cry; I tried to avoid asking her those questions that would tell me who lived behind the still-beautiful face and the gay, pleasant talk.

But I wanted to know—and I wanted very much for her to know me.

One afternoon, after she'd just bought some new bedroom furniture, I was sitting on the floor in her room, following her instructions on how to put shelf paper properly on the insides of bureau drawers. That had never occurred to me; I'd always put my family's clothes on the bare wood.

"Why do you do this, Mama?" I asked.

"Just to make things nicer. I always did it," she said. "Don't you remember, baby? You always had shelf paper in your drawers at home."

I laughed and told her I'd never noticed. "But why didn't you ever teach me any of this?"

She told me that she'd always found all housekeeping moderately unpleasant, and that anyone with any sense would feel the same. "The best thing," she said, "is to marry someone who did well enough that you could get someone to do it for you."

I told her that, as we both knew, I hadn't; but I felt I had a very good life just the same. I tried to describe how we lived in Emporia, what it was like to be a faculty wife, how it was in an "intellectual community"—which it indeed seemed to me at the time. I told her about the people we knew and the kind of parties we had, about the concerts and plays we attended; it was very different from what her life had always been.

"I always thought," she said, "that you'd marry an Army officer, Judy." Just as she had—*twice*. We laughed about that. She had prepared me for that role. She lifted herself slightly from the pillow and looked over at me where I sat on the floor, folding shelf paper. "I thought you were well-suited to being an Army officer's wife." She paused. "Just the same, I know you and John are happy together. I want you to be happy, baby, and to have a good marriage." She talked about the work that took, how much love and self-sacrifice. I should pay more attention to John's career; my chief obligations, aside from Kathleen, were to John. I could be a great help to him by entertaining and looking nice, meeting the right people, looking for more ways to help him.

*In Hamilton*, I thought, *those were your choices: you were either married or pathetic. And if you were married, your husband came first.*

Her husband had always come first. My father and then my stepfather—and their careers—were her chief interests. She'd played endless rubbers of bridge, given and gone to just as many cocktail parties and receptions. The perfect Army wife.

She had been a fantastic hostess, and loved nothing better than having great hordes of people to dinner. She was always so gay, so pretty, always so charming. For a long time I had thought that was what life was all about.

But she had been a strong person, too, who, because she was an Army wife and left alone a lot, had to be both mother and father. She had had to learn how to take care of a car and maintain it, how to pack and move by herself, how to shield her husbands and her children in a thousand emotional ways.

She had learned how to be self-sacrificing, and she had tried to teach it pretty thoroughly to me.

She told me that she was worried about my budding enthusiasm for a career of my own. "You'll get too involved with your work," she warned. "You'll be too tired. You'll neglect John and Kathleen. Working mothers are away from home too much."

I tried to explain to her that I had found being interested in something else made me happier and so a better person at home, that teaching would not keep me away that much, and anyway, we needed the money. I tried to assure her that I *did* work hard at my marriage.

Soon after I had returned to Emporia, my mother-in-law called to say they'd taken my mother back to the hospital and though she hadn't been told anything specific, she had the feeling Mama couldn't last much longer. She thought I should come right away.

I stayed with my mother that night and watched as, slowly and painfully, she died.

My stepfather and brother were inconsolable; they were both paralyzed with grief. Every decision that had to be made only brought them fresh pain; I made as many of the arrangements without them as I could. When the doctor wanted to do an autopsy, Papa and Dick were adamant against it; I had to convince them that Mama would have wanted it, it might help someone else.

John and I took care of all the small details of the funeral arrangements, too. My stepfather insisted that the coffin be left open, but when he saw the tasteless way they had made Mama up, he became terribly upset again.

That wasn't her! She looked different, *different*. He couldn't stand it; it had to be fixed.

I would have done anything to make him feel just a little better, so I went back to that apartment where she had spent the last few weeks of her life, and looked for her cosmetics.

In the drawers, her clothes still smelled like her.

Then I went to the funeral home, where my mother lay. Carefully I took off the make-up they'd put on her and then slowly, carefully, began to apply her own. I tried to ignore one of the funeral directors who came along with me, who chatted amiably and matter-of-factly about the problems of making dead people look "natural."

Didn't he know who I was?

Didn't he know that she was my *mother*, for chrissake?

Maybe he thought I didn't care. I didn't cry in public the way Papa and Dick did, but if I didn't, it wasn't because it didn't hurt. It hurt terribly. Awfully. Mingled with deep feelings of regret and frustration.

I knew the tears were in there somewhere, but I held them back.

"Will you please leave or shut up?" I told the funeral director coldly. He remained, but silently.

I wondered if I'd ever feel the same about wearing make-up again. I realized, sadly, how seldom I had ever seen my mother when she didn't have on her mask; she had never gone anywhere without her "face" on.

*Why?* It was so silly, so pointless. *She was such a beautiful woman. She had such lovely, regular features.* I'd always wished I'd looked just like her. *She would have been even more beautiful,* I thought, *without any of this stupid cosmetic gunk.*

Why had she felt she needed it? Had it been some kind of protection for her? As I looked down at her face, and touched it lightly, I wondered who my mother really was. I didn't know.

I had spent most of my life with her, but I didn't really know who this woman was. The make-up had been part of her protection. And smiles and certain words and a thousand gestures—and, oh, so much more. My eyes were wet now.

She had been "my mother" to me. I had always seen her and loved her as that. But she was her own person, too. *There are whole areas of your life, your mind,* I thought, looking down at her, *that I never knew anything about.* My hands were beginning to shake and I knew the tears were very close. I quickly gathered up the tubes and jars and boxes, dropped them into her cosmetic case, and took my leave of that awful room. *Now I never will.*

# 10

## "What You Need Is a Good Lay!"

When Mama bought me a ukelele for my twelfth birthday and taught me how to play it, I never dreamed that frivolous skill would prove so useful.

A friend of mine, who knew they were looking for someone to teach a few courses, suggested I see the chairman of the art department at Kansas State Teachers College. She didn't tell me that the old buzzard had played honkytonk piano in his youth, or that the department had an informal jazz band. One of the first questions he asked when he interviewed me for the job was whether I played a musical instrument.

"Sure. Cello," I said.

He snorted with disgust. "No, not *that*. Can't you play something else?"

I told him I played the ukelele. His face brightened and he said: "Hey, that's terrific."

So I dusted off my uke and joined the art department. My first assignment was to teach three sections of the required art appreciation course for freshmen, and despite the criminally low salary, I leaped at the chance.

I loved teaching right away. It was tremendously satisfying and I knew it was the work I had been looking for. Kathleen was not overly impressed with either my enthusiasm or the job itself; she knew lots of teachers. "That's nothing," she told me; "Melanie's mother is a meter maid and she gets to wear a *uni*-form!" But teaching challenged, excited, and thrilled me.

John had finished his thesis and finally got his EdD. The dissertation had dominated our life for years. We had invested our emotions and funneled all our energies into that project. My entire life, it seemed, had been wrapped up in this thing, and it was something over which I had no control. I must have read John's dissertation four hundred times; I edited part of it; I typed all the rough drafts; I became so involved that I insulated John completely, so he would have no worries while he worked.

Once Kathleen went off to buy some breakfast milk at the grocery six blocks away and wasn't found for four hours. I called the police, frantic—and a description was broadcast over the local radio station. While I paced and fretted, a dozen friends called to ask if they could help, to offer support. Even when the police finally found her clear across town, I refused to wake John, who had worked late the night before and needed his sleep.

And on the day he had his orals, I came home, ate lunch with him, wished him well with the last half of his exams, and only later that night told him that I had been in a car wreck that morning.

When I watched the president of the university place that long blue hood around John's shoulders, I felt a huge weight had been lifted from my own, and I probably wept more with relief than joy.

Had it been worth all the effort?

The raise he'd been promised did come through—but I think he had misunderstood the chairman: he must have said "substandard," not "substantial."

Worse, that pattern of insulating, protecting John, became one of the strongest legacies of the dissertation; it took me years to break that habit.

The Nelson Gallery in Kansas City has a fine collection of Oriental art. There are only a handful of paintings in America from the period on which I was doing my master's thesis—the refined and artificial court life whose main value was esthetics as depicted in Lady Murasaki's *Tale of Genji*. The Nelson Gallery had one of them and an adequate Oriental art library besides. I'd drive the sixty miles to Kansas City on the weekends, and spend the day with the card catalog in the basement—a creepy labyrinth of dark corridors that made me expect to meet Lon Chaney trailing his mummy-rags.

Back home, I'd sit down at the typewriter and John would say: "Honey, where are my socks?"

I'd tell him, then when he still couldn't find them, I'd get up, get them for him, sit down again and type a few lines. He'd call: "Did you pick up my shirts from the laundry?"

Was he going to interrupt me every whipstitch?

"Look, I'm trying to finish my thesis. Remember when you were doing yours? You were *never* interrupted."

"I know, Judy," he said. "Look, it's wrong, and I'll try harder not to . . ."

But a day later, it was the socks and the shirts again, or the *TV Guide*, or the keys to the car. When I reminded him, he said: "God, I didn't mean to do that"—and I don't think he did, not consciously.

John had always encouraged me in my work, and when I began to teach, it revitalized and strengthened our relationship. I was doing something that he did, that he did well, and I had a two-pronged fascination with it: the subject matter and the discipline of teaching itself. The material I had to learn myself, and did so with pleasure—and John and I talked constantly about the mechanics of teaching: how to do it, how to be most effective.

John was delighted with my interest—with the stories I brought back from the classroom and the increasing reports that, to my absolute joy, people thought I was becoming a good teacher.

He was less delighted with my writing. He read the first chapter of my thesis and made fun of it. I knew it was good, and had received high praise from my major professor on it. I never let him see the rest of it.

Nor did he like the art column I'd begun to do for the Emporia *Gazette*. He read a few columns and found the sentences too long, my references too obscure, my punctuation peculiar indeed.

"Well, the paper loves it, and my colleagues tell me it's great, and the town likes it."

He said: "Good for you. But it sounds awful to me."

"Well, just don't read it anymore," I said. "I don't need to hear that."

So be it. I really wasn't asking him to love my work, or to do my socks for me—only to *let* me work, to leave me alone.

It was asking a lot, apparently.

All that winter, while snow was ass-high to a tall Indian and I tried desperately to find enough quiet moments to do my work, the household and its demands never let up. I began to resent the intrusions. Perhaps John couldn't help what he did; perhaps he simply did not respect what I was doing. Or had he forgotten, if he'd ever known, how to take care of himself?

There's another possibility, which I've been reluctant to accept: that he resented my new success. Did he feel that my career was becoming more important to me than the household was, than he was—that he had to squelch it?

That last summer in Denton, when I was finishing my thesis and preparing for my oral exams, I remember having the distinct impression that he was sabotaging me. He called me the night before I took my orals, and could not have missed the nervousness in my voice. I needed cheering up—badly.

"Oh, by the way," he said, "I ran into Jack from the art department. It looks like you may have lost your job for next year."

"Terrific!" I said. "Just what I needed to hear."

"He's not positive."

"What are you doing to me?" I asked, disbelieving.

"Nothing," he protested.

As it turned out I had not lost my job, but I spent a bad night worrying about the prospect, and only just pulled out in time to take my orals.


We had been hoarding money maniacally, and looking for a house that we could buy. With both of us working, we'd been able to at last amass a down payment.

In Hamilton, what mattered was the family you were from—much more than the amount of money you had or where you lived. There were a lot of kids in school with me whose parents were better off than ours, but were still not in "our circle." You had to be Old Family; you had to have lived in Hamilton since the Flood.

In Emporia, money stood for something, but people

spent less and didn't seem to enjoy their spending; some of the richest people in town lived in little old dinky houses and drove old cars. There was no sense of extravagance or display among the "best citizens" of Emporia, and most of the women I knew had little interest in fashion; their looks had all jelled in the style that was prevalent when they married, no matter what that might have been. You gained status in that puritanical community by being a good citizen, attending church regularly, and participating in community affairs.

I couldn't become a conservative Republican, which would have been best, but since Democrats were scarce, I proved my good citizenship by poll-watching at elections. We attended Episcopal church services religiously, and I was active in church affairs: so we were flawless there. I went to the Faculty Wives Club, and I wrote the art column, was a board member of the Emporia Friends of Art, and helped with the Mobile Art Unit that brought culture to nine Kansas counties.

I was conscious of doing it all to enhance John's position at the school and in the town. He hadn't asked, but he appreciated it.

Ultimately, though, you were not taken seriously unless you owned a house. Preferably one you'd paid cash for. All cash. Which we could never do.

It was better to have a house *in front* of the country club among the older houses. Behind the club, the houses were as expensive, but all *new;* they simply didn't carry the same prestige.

One day on that last summer in Denton, John called me and said: "I don't think we're ever going to find a house that we can afford, Judy. Maybe we ought to take the money and go to Europe."

"Great," I said. I'd always wanted to go; there was so

much I'd been longing to see. So the next day I mailed off my passport for renewal.

John called again about a week later, and I could tell immediately that he was bubbling inside. "I've got a surprise for you," he said. "I've bought you a house."

"A house?"

"I hope you like it—because I've already signed the papers." As he proceeded to tell me all about the house he'd bought for me, I could tell he was absolutely tickled with what he'd done.

"Well, if I don't like it," I said, "I'll never tell you. How's that?"

John had bought *more* than a house: the Sullivans now owned one of Emporia's "stately homes." I was dumbstruck when I got home and saw it for the first time: it was a big, white, two-story Colonial house on Sherwood Way, in the posh old country-club section of town, with a large, terraced yard with lots of big elm trees. From the day we moved in I had a fantasy that I didn't really live there, that someday I'd see the true owner come floating down the stairs. And it would be Myrna Loy.

I liked the house but never felt it was mine. In 1932, when it was finished, it had been featured in *Better Homes and Gardens*. It was a beautifully designed American Colonial—a style of architecture that abounds in Darien, Connecticut, and the posher suburbs of the Midwest. It looked like Andy Hardy's girlfriend's house. The first story was fieldstone; the second, white clapboard. Green shutters on the windows and a green roof. A curving fieldstone walk led to the solid front door, embellished with some tasteful brass and flanked by a pair of towering junipers.

The entry hall was impressive: a room in itself with an

elegantly curving staircase and a brass chandelier. The walls were papered in beige with a soft-gold medallion design that I wanted to change. The door led to a service hall, with the kitchen and a half-bath, and another outside door to the attached garage.

John had warned me about the profusion of doors, also the colors of the bathrooms and kitchen.

"What color are they? What does it look like?" I asked by telephone from Denton, Texas, about this house I'd never laid eyes on.

"You know what blood bait looks like? Well, that's the color."

He was right, too.

The dining room was the prettiest room in the house. For one thing, it was the only room we could completely furnish. We painted the walls and woodwork white and covered the windows with white silk. I upholstered the valances for the big windows that looked out over the stone patio in the back of the house and the terraced lawn. A pair of T'ang Dynasty reproductions mounted on silk decorated the walls on either side of the big window and I covered the dining room chairs with a pale apricot silk. A small, crystal chandelier reflected in the polished mahogany of my mother's dining room table and the glass of the big breakfront, where I stored all the silver.

The living room still had a way to go. Freshly painted and also draped all in white, it was proportioned generously and had an elegant fireplace whose mantel was a reproduction of one in my book of *Southern Interiors*. There was a small, screened porch off the living room.

Upstairs, the large center-hall staircase opened on either end to two immense bedrooms, and a guest room that Kathleen eventually took over for her own. In it, she had her canopied bed, several ancient chests of drawers, and a small desk. The walls were covered with posters, the chests held her aquariums and record player, and every other flat surface was thoroughly upholstered with papers, drawings, books, records, clothes. It also contained a mammoth puppet theater; and lengthy, impromptu puppet shows were a regular feature on rainy days.

The architect, a fellow parishioner at St. Andrew's, said he was happy we had the house: we seemed to belong in it.

But I never felt that way.

It had cost far more than we could afford, and John's small down payment had left us with a large mortgage; and it needed a good deal of work besides. I always felt at war with the place, that it was going to get control of me if I didn't control it. John said, much later, there was a hex on the house.

But it was good, after all the tight rooms we'd lived in, to spread out. Besides Kathleen's bedroom, we had an extra bedroom upstairs that was always filled with some indigent student or itinerant friend. In the spring and summer, we liked to eat breakfast out on the porch, looking out over our back and side yards with the full shade trees and flower beds, laughing at our old cat Smoky being dive-bombed by the grackles.

I spent a great deal of time in the house—servicing the house. But I spent a lot of hours down in the basement, too. The basement was full of rooms, perhaps originally planned to house servants; we used one for storage, another as the laundry room. Under the living room was a den, pine paneled and with a fireplace, that I used as a place to read and study. John built me a desk and some bookshelves and I kept the typewriter there. There was ample room to spread out papers and clippings, to save all the art magazines I subscribed to, and to prepare my lectures. It was the least pretty, the least promising part of the whole house, but it was my favorite. It was very quiet in the basement; "Mama's dungeon," Kathleen called it.

When you live in a place like that you feel some obligation to live up to it. We tried. Because it was so huge we could entertain, and we began to hold lots of parties. On the Fourth of July the nearby country club always had a fireworks display: our front lawn was a regular ringside seat. So we always had people over—with their children— for a barbecue. We would sit on the lawn on quilts, drinking beer and watching the rockets and Roman candles explode in the dark sky. And on the night of the annual faculty art department show, it became a ritual for us to invite all the people in the art and education departments (oil and water), some of our favorite students, and everybody else in town to whom we'd ever taken a fancy— everyone from a most distinguished judge to the town drunk, about two hundred and fifty in all.

(My friend Anne, who taught in the art department with me, now holds the party every year on the night of the faculty show.)

John bought me an MG to zip around in, and there was plenty of zipping to do—Kathleen had to be ferried to Girl Scouts, teeth-straightening, play practice, trombone lessons; I drove to Wichita, Topeka, and Kansas City to write up museum doings for my column in the *Gazette;* as always, I ran the house—all five hundred rooms of it; and I taught nearly a full schedule of art classes at the college.

At first I was perfectly content with the art department—deeply committed to teaching and delighted to be there; but as I look back at it now, I realize that I was

never really a colleague, which was how I fancied myself
then. At faculty meetings, Anne and I brought homemade
coffee cake or cookies to go with the secretary's coffee—it
was expected and we did it. The men in our department
either patronized, teased, or ridiculed us; they never
treated us as equals.

We were shorted on our salaries. Anne was the lowest
paid instructor in the department; I wasn't even on the
scale. A full schedule was nine teaching hours—I was
always assigned eight and so got paid two-thirds of base
salary. They were reluctant to hire faculty wives full-time.
Anne, whose children were very young, preferred to
take the lower salary in lieu of the extra responsibilities of
committee work and more advisees, but I was not at all
happy.

The angrier I got, the easier it became to say so. We
had to demand equal responsibility, I thought, if we could
ever hope—and the possibility seemed dim—to someday
get equal salary and promotions. It was so bloody unfair—
and I could see that if I didn't stand up for myself and
learn to fight I'd be thoroughly run over. A couple of
times I was.

My first office, in a condemned portion of the old art
building, had a wasps' nest over my desk that none of the
custodians would remove; I finally did it myself. When
the new art building was finished, Anne and I shared an
office, which we were happy to do since we liked each
other. I would never have given a thought to the office assignment if I had not been told it had been made to "avoid
problems."

What problems?

The men were the problems, not us. One of the committee members would sit with his feet up on his desk and

shout through the outer office: "Sullivan! Get your fine high ass in here!" When I pretended not to hear, his secretary would come to my door and say politely, with cheeks blazing: "Mrs. Sullivan, I think Mr. McNeil would like to see you if you have a moment."

Once he called me into his office and shut the door at once; there was another male colleague there, and they both seemed nervous about something. They shuffled their feet, fidgeted about, looked at each other and out the window, and then one of them blurted: "We gotta ask you something."

"Okay, what?" I said.

"You ask her."

"No, you do it."

I looked from one to the other, bewildered.

"Well," one of them said, "what we want to know is . . . is Everts knocked up again?"

They were referring to Anne, who had recently given birth and still had a bit of a tummy. I was speechless.

"We keep a close eye on you broads," threw in McNeil, giving me a wink. I was so angry I shouted: "I don't know and if I did I wouldn't tell you bastards!"

*Their* women, the *best* kind of women, for the most part were interested in doing something arty—like weaving or throwing pots; their women liked to stay home and bake bread and have lots of children. Earth-mother types. That's what they liked to think. I knew those women, they were my friends. I knew better. The men couldn't understand why I wouldn't do the same. When they enrolled twenty more students in one of my classes than I had seats for, and I came storming in, as I did with more and more frequency, they'd sneer: "What's the matter with you? Got your period?" Or they'd say I should stay

home and have more children. One of them summed it up
once and for all: "You need a good lay."

My hostility grew. An African student, to whom I'd
given the "B" he earned instead of the "A" he wanted, told
me: "How dare you, a *woman*, do this to me?" At a national conference, a famous scholar sitting next to me introduced himself: "And what do you do, my dear?" He
leaned over, saw my tag, and read aloud, "Ah, Judith
Sullivan. Art history. Emporia State Teachers College.
Emporia, Kansas." The whole thing broke him up. When
he'd recovered from his laughing fit, he picked me up by
the arm and dragged me all over the room, introducing me
to people—several of them men whose books I used as
texts. "Look at this charming child," he'd say. "Imagine,
she teaches art history in Emporia, Kansas!" They all
seemed to find that a real knee-slapper. When my first column for the *Gazette* appeared, chopped to pieces and
under the byline, "Mrs. John B. Sullivan," I complained
to the editor: "Mrs. John B. Sullivan could be practically
anybody! As a matter of fact, it's also my mother-in-law!
My name is Judith T. Sullivan!"

"It's against the paper's policy, Judy."

"You use Ann Landers' by-line and you'll use mine or
you can forget the whole thing," I said, summoning a
force I hadn't known I possessed. "And furthermore, I
want you to run every word I give you—the whole column. Everything I say and just the way I say it. If you
don't know what the big words mean, look them up in the
dictionary."

Kathleen was doing well in school. She had become a
good reader and was particularly skilled in creative crafts.
I tried, with all my busyness, to be home from work every

afternoon by the time she returned from school. I liked to sit down with her, drink a Pepsi, munch some Cheetos and have a good visit. Afterward, we'd make something together or play with one of the cats. We always had lots of animals in the house—two or three cats at a time, birds, fishes, and an old crawfish named Clarabelle, who lived with us a great many years until she met her end beneath a tumbled rock.

I had no more crying spells because I had significant work to do and was somehow finding the time to do it all. Between John and me, we were making a fairly comfortable living now, but the expenses of the house were astronomical. I added two days and six more hours of classes at Washburn University—sixty miles away in Topeka—to my already busy schedule; I began to do more writing, get grants for further research, and travel more often to professional conferences. I noticed that John began to minimize, even frivolize what I was doing, saying things like, "Well, your salary just about pays the taxes." I'd ask him why he had to talk about it in those terms—and I could sense that we had become, in this and in other ways, competitive. I was becoming successful—in my work and as a person—and though he outwardly encouraged me, he was somehow bugged by it all.

I was elected a delegate to the national convention of the American Association of University Professors that year, and went off to Washington, DC, delighted with the opportunity for the trip. The convention was rich with eye-opening surprises. When a woman made a resolution from the floor about improving the salaries of women professors, everyone nodded solemnly, did nothing, and then passed on to another resolution condemning Hungary for squelching academic freedom, which they discussed for hours. I met women at that convention who were light years ahead of me in their academic training and in their thinking about the predicament of women in the academic world. The pinch is always individual; you think it's happening only to you, that you're unlucky or inadequately prepared. But then you see women who have all these things you think you need to make you all right, and they're no better off.

At Emporia State it was the same. Oh, there were two women who were supposedly treated properly. One was an associate professor of biology, whose research was responsible for most of the government money that came into the school. Another was an extremely well-qualified woman in the Spanish department. "If you were as well-qualified as these women," administration spokesmen said, "you'd be as well paid."

When the AAUP salary study came out, we all discovered that even these women's salaries—these exceptional women—were below those of their less qualified male colleagues.

The English department would have been paralyzed if it could not exploit faculty wives for the teaching of freshman English, at shamefully low salaries. Academic serfs. And they all taught, at those crumby wages, without complaining. In most cases they had put a man through college, taken care of his house and children, worked at odd, hard hours to get an advanced degree of their own, and now were being further penalized because they were women.

*Women.* Yes, being a woman meant so much more than I had ever realized. It began to explain so much.

In a tentative way I began to see it as a political question, though I didn't read a single book or article on women's rights during those years, nor as a history major had I ever really learned anything about the nineteenth-century women's movement.

Women *were* severely underpaid in the universities, in addition to the less tangible, more subtle ways they were mistreated. But the men in the AAUP took that fact no more seriously than my department took my gripes.

*"You need a good lay."*

I tried to storm out of meetings, like I'd seen the men do so effectively. But when I did it they all just assumed I was going to the ladies' room!

Going to meetings, taking on more responsibility at school, was exciting; but it also complicated my life. There was still the big house to care for—with help only a half day a week—and playing the accomplished hostess as well as wife and mother. I lived deeply in teaching and research, was so excited by that bigger world I began to resent the hours and energy I had to spend on housework and entertaining. I began to schedule my time with absolute precision. I had to. My purse was always crammed with the endless lists that kept me on top of things: shopping lists, errand lists, work lists. The better organized I was, the more time I had for those activities that gave me life.

Perhaps it was the pressure, but for the first time I began to have fantasy-dreams that something had happened to Kathleen and John—that I was free.

For years, on and off, I had these uncontrollable dreams. I told no one about them; I felt too guilty.

In the spring of 1968, I saw a notice on the bulletin board that the National Endowment for the Humanities was funding a series of workshops in Negro universities all over the country, in an effort to prepare interested people of various disciplines to teach the new black studies courses that were springing up everywhere. One, in art and literature, would be held at Southern University in Baton Rouge, Louisiana.

When the chairman, at one of the departmental meetings, asked if anyone wanted to go, his question was greeted with mass apathy. Most of the artists used the summers to work.

I had followed, with some sadness, the fruits of the civil rights movement. Some of the laws that had been passed weren't being implemented; integration, even in Kansas, was often a farce; the laws had been changed but not people's minds. The good feeling between blacks and whites of the early 1960s had given way to a bitter militancy that strictly excluded whites. Knowing I was no longer welcome in the fight, I had plunged headlong into my own discipline—trying to learn it, trying to teach it. But the problems were still there. Black students in my classes wanted to know, "Who *are* the black artists?" I didn't know; I could only think of a few. Were there more? What work were they doing?

"Me," I told the chairman. "I'd like to go to Baton Rouge."

He looked over at me and smiled. "I was going to suggest you, Sullivan," he said. "You're the only one here who speaks that darky language."

I went to Baton Rouge for two consecutive summers. The first summer was interesting, even compelling; the second affected me much more profoundly. Before I left Emporia that second summer, I had recurring dreams that I would never return.

In a sense, I never did.

# 11

## Late to the Revolution

I remember Baton Rouge with great clarity. How we'd walk along the old Mississippi to breakfast in the early mornings, as the sun rose and burned off the fog. I can see the fog lifting from the river, the huge trees with Spanish moss hanging from them, and feel the *physicality* of the place—the humidity that kept my hair so damp I thought it was sure to mildew, the heat you could not escape.

I can remember how we never slept more than a few hours but were always intensely awake.

I can remember the people: Colson, with his ponderous body and agile mind, who could recite African poetry so movingly he'd cry himself, along with most of his audience; O'Brien, superbrilliant, sharp, revolutionary, on literature and life; Schwitters, this southern belle's first contact with what Dr. Sanchez called a "clever Jewish intellectual," who had black bushy eyebrows and big beard to match, and old raggedy clothes that hung like a sack around his dumpy figure. And a black woman—a PhD in literature who, all day, would be eloquent, informed, articulate, but when evening fell would shout: "*Hooo-whoo-eee!* It's six o'clock and I've turned into a nigger."

It is hard, even now, to understand precisely what happened to me in Baton Rouge—to chart its electrifying effect on my mind.

At thirty-three, I was still in many ways the nice lady everyone had always wanted me to be, had trained me to be. I had "turned out" rather well. Arguments and unpleasantness were a regrettable necessity sometimes at work; but for most situations, I much preferred smiling and fluttering my eyelashes, would rather soothe than disturb. My southern radar told me that the independent notions I was beginning to have, and worse, to express, were just that—disturbing.

The only really independent women I'd known were old eccentrics—harmless mavericks toward whom the community could afford to be tolerant. Why not, for heaven's sake? They were no threat. But I had admired them for their independent spirits and I realize now that all my life, in a quiet way, I had been a maverick and a scrapper too—but one taught that it was unladylike to fight. I'd wanted to play Tarzan with the boys, I'd refused a debut, I'd hunted with my husband and his friends—but my life essentially had been a southern odyssey: I'd come from the right family, I'd married the right man, I'd lived in the right house on the right street. Even my mild flirtation with civil rights at college, a few summers on my own, hardly had changed the fact that in 1969 I was innocent, even backward. Maybe what actually happened at Baton Rouge was not much different from any intense college experience—being exposed to fresh and dynamic minds for the first time, dramatically new ideas, having the sense of new worlds opening every day. It happens to some people at eighteen or twenty or twenty-five; it happened to me at thirty-three but my reaction was no less authentic. In fact, some sense of quite how old I was, how much I'd been missing, probably made Baton Rouge even more cataclysmic. I'd been precocious at nothing but marrying.

Compound that with the wet heat, the pressure-cooker atmosphere, the fact that it was 1969, and I can understand it even better.

Astrologers spoke of a strange conjunction of the planets that summer. Americans walked on the moon. Some went to Woodstock. After that came Kent State and Jackson State, Cambodia and the student strikes. Revolution, of many varieties, was in the air. For me, a very vulnerable southern woman, it occurred in a place called Baton Rouge.

Part of my reaction, no doubt, was heightened by my sheltered childhood. Part of it was caused by breaking out of my shell for the first time, getting a crash course in the twentieth century. But I discovered not only a brave new world outside me but one essentially *inside* me. I had spent years and years without self-confidence—keeping house, taking care of my daughter, helping my husband through graduate school. Something—ambition or clairvoyance—kept me going to school, doing it left-handedly, a few courses at a time: it had taken me six years to finish my bachelor's degree, four my master's. Economic need kept me working and boredom made me try to scrounge up better and more interesting jobs wherever I found myself in the wake of John's career.

I'd always felt valueless, dependent on John for everything—ideas, the way I lived my life. I was nothing; then he married me and made me something. I'd lived in him:

trying to keep abreast of his studies, typing his papers, a constant helpmeet. He decided where and when we moved, what house we lived in, everything.

Then, in Baton Rouge, I listened to certain other people—but I also began listening to myself. I didn't exactly turn into a different person, I just became more the person I should have been all along—and one who had no business at all being where she found herself. When that happened, *nothing* could ever be more important. I would do *anything* to protect what I'd found, and I suddenly discovered I'd gained the tools I'd always lacked—in Hamilton, in San Antonio, in Emporia: tools with which to think.

How could I ever know that would mean one day giving up my husband and child?

The first summer had been interesting, exciting, but not cataclysmic. Colson, Schwitters, and O'Brien were there then. And the program had been administered then, too, by Professor James Horton, dean, scholar, writer—with an ebullient sense of humor and a big walrus moustache. There had been about forty of us in literature and art; black literature had been accessible, but no one knew much about the art. There were only two books on the subject—one by an English anthropologist, written in the early 1950s, and the other a sketchy volume, long out-of-print. How could you find the black artists—not by their names or by their work—and what *was* black art? Was there such a thing as a black esthetic? I became intrigued by the problem and threw myself into the research completely.

We often talked late into the night and I found myself, perhaps for the first time, accepted as someone who had something to contribute—not simply because of my growing knowledge of black art, but because of my insights about people, my ideas.

I came back to Emporia all fired up after that first summer and began a long year of heavy research—compiling a major bibliography on black art, making and acquiring a comprehensive slide collection, corresponding with Horton and other scholars across the country.

I worked hard all that year—but it was always work that had to be sandwiched between my two jobs, the unending series of parties that John loved so much, the folderol; between chauffering Kathleen and tending to that elaborate house on Sherwood Way.

Why couldn't we just live more simply—and more cooperatively?

John and I were very close that year. He was heavily involved with the politics of the college now; I spent a lot of time sitting by the fireplace in our living room, doing needlepoint and listening to him go on, thoughtfully, patiently, about the president's intentions and what strategies to expect. I was becoming expert at college politics and politicking, and found that my instincts—southern radar?—could be a real help to my husband.

I became more reflective that year. I looked at the women around me, the quality of their lives, the values we all lived by. One neighbor with three children stayed at home all day and drank; two others had been in and out of mental institutions. One night, standing alone in a back hallway at a party, where I'd gone to escape the smoke and the noise, I heard the husband of one of my friends talking about an investment club he belonged to that met once a week at a local motel; the men, many of whom I knew, met, drank, and balled girls from the college—those were the weekly meetings, it seemed. I stood in the shadows of the hallway, trapped where they couldn't see me.

I heard only the voices—sordid, repulsive.

I waited until long after the voices stopped before I came out, but when I did, he was still there and he saw me and knew I knew.

These people were more affluent than those in San Antonio, and had more mobility; but the same pathology reigned. They were bored. They were trying to escape from the boredom that I saw built into so many families around me, particularly in small towns and isolated sections of larger towns. It was harder for the women, and it troubled me to see the quality of so many of their lives, tied to the house, finding their diversions in buying still more clothes or redecorating their overdecorated houses, or living vicariously through a husband or through their children—or having an affair. Energies spent in strange ways; abilities wasted and frivolized. I knew one woman who antiqued the whole outside of her eight-room house.

I didn't want to be like them.

Increasingly, I didn't want any part of that life.

A new chairman was elected to the art department in Emporia, and it became clear to me at once that my position was in jeopardy. I was not the kind of woman he wanted. I was too uppity.

In January I was scheduled to be sent to the College Art Association meeting in Boston, but the new chairman informed me a week before the trip: "I'm going in your place."

"That's been promised to me," I protested, "and I'm going."

"You're part-time," he said. "You're a faculty wife."

"Look, this is my trip."

"Well, the president told me I can't send you. There's nothing I can do about it."

"That's a barefaced lie. If you want to go yourself, pay for it yourself. With your salary, you can afford it."

Fury made short work of my Miz Lady. The injustice prompted me to match my language to his. "If you have any balls at all," I raged on, "you'll go tell the president you promised this trip to me five months ago, and you're going to honor that promise!"

That did it. As soon as the president got rung in, it was all over. The next day, I was called in for another "conference" with the new chairman.

"Well, I spoke to the president." He wouldn't look me in the eye. "You can have the trip to Boston, but he said to tell you that your contract would not be renewed next fall."

So I was fired. And since I was, I decided I might as well give him the benefit of my sentiments on the subject.

I did—and then went home and cried. What would we do without that part of my salary next year? John said we'd find a way to manage—after all, I still had the Washburn job. He was as furious as I was and ready to raise hell in all directions, but he and the president had enough differences as it was. Besides, I didn't want him fighting my fights for me anymore. Getting fired turned out to be a liberating experience.

I had been excited that first year when I first heard about Baton Rouge. I'd rushed home to John and told him I really wanted to go. The neighbors might think, "The sun starts shining hard and Judy's going to split," but John looked over the papers and said, "I don't see why you shouldn't go. Kathleen's anxious to return to camp, and this will be an interesting experience, and good for your career. I'll get along all right," he said smiling. "The department wives will parcel out the dinner invitations again, I'll miss you and the house will get to be a mess— but I won't starve."

He was just as accommodating the next summer when I was invited back. But this time *I* did not want to return to Baton Rouge. I had taught the first summer session at Emporia State and I was tired. I only wanted to stay home and get the house straightened, ready for school in the fall; I'd be teaching northern Renaissance art at Washburn in the fall, a new subject. Worse, I began having recurrent nightmares filled with violence: I was running in the dark, I saw that long stretch of road when you enter the university grounds, with the football field on one side, the ditch, the swamp, and the jungle on the other. I became more terrified as real violence came to Baton Rouge. Several weeks before I was to leave, bad trouble hit. The National Guard was in Scotlandville, the suburb that contained the university—two young blacks had been shot in the back.

Finally I went to see my priest, Ted, a close friend. "I'm really scared," I told him.

"So, don't go, Judy," he counseled. "You don't *have* to, you know."

"Yes, I do," I said. "You don't understand. I *do* have to go, I'm committed to it. To back out now would be just plain cowardly." By that time the troops were in Scotlandville; I dreamed of gunshots, of running for my life, of being mauled by police dogs. "I'm scared to death," I said, "but I wouldn't even consider not going. I wanted . . . I only wanted to check in with someone—to say I'm scared." I looked around the familiar office. On the wall were the purple hearts Ted had earned as a chaplain in Vietnam, and a color photograph of the chopper he used to have to ride. He kept the photograph to remind him how hard it was to make yourself do some things. For him, getting into that helicopter to fly into a combat zone was one of those extra tough numbers. We looked at the picture together. "Okay," he said, smiling, "I'll pray for you all the time you're gone."

Fine. Good. But I still put all my affairs in order before I left.

Everything about the second summer was different, from the fears with which it began to the new person I was when I returned.

My paranoia reached its peak on the plane, which is why I called Horton from the airport instead of trying to persuade a taxi driver to take me to Scotlandville. I was astounded when he told me on the drive from the airport that he'd named me to chair the art section. "Judy, I want you to run it for me."

Then the fear receded and I suddenly began to think of practical problems, and who would be back. It was a breathtaking challenge. The work had begun.

That part of the conference, running the art section, was enormously satisfying—discovering I had something to say, to which people I admired wanted to listen. Midway through, we presented a program for the literature people, and they were well-pleased with my paper. I pushed myself beyond all previous limits—that was part of what happened at Baton Rouge: I did a satisfying piece of work *by myself*.

Those Denton summers had begun to change the low estimate I had of myself—the sad sense of worthlessness and dependence. Alone, I had begun to see myself as a person with certain abilities, certain potentialities; there was perhaps something there that could be *myself.* Now, as the work of the conference went on, I felt compartments open in me that I had not known were there.

Something else was happening that summer, too. I was reaching out to make a vital connection with people who thought and felt as I did. I had always felt there was some special way of latching on, of making contact. For a while, I thought the way was marriage and motherhood, and then it was teaching. Suddenly none of that was enough. There seemed to be something outside me very big, terribly valid, that I needed to be a part of.

There was an electricity in the air. We had all been identifying more and more with our students, less and less with the structure. We were breaking open new paths. I was very thrilled with it all—the work I was doing, the stature I had, the burning urgency every minute of every hot, wet day.

We worked all day and then spent the evenings, from after dinner to the wee small hours of the morning, talking. We drank vast amounts of vodka and beer, and when the dorm food paled we made runs into Scotlandville for chicken and dirty rice—rice cooked in chicken grease, with lots of pepper thrown in.

I achieved a kind of metaphysical state.

I was eating practically nothing, sleeping no more than four or five hours a night, surviving on cigarettes and vodka and a little dirty rice, and I had more energy and felt better than I ever had. I felt light-headed and supercharged.

The people around me liked me for precisely those idiosyncratic qualities, those independent thoughts, that everyone else liked me *in spite of*. They didn't like me for the things I did for them, or for what they wanted me to be: they liked me for the things I liked in myself.

The sessions were often tense, hostile, partisan. I gave a paper and someone stood up and loudly denounced me as a communist. "Anyone who's spent as much money at Neiman Marcus as I have," I shouted back, "couldn't possibly be a communist." Schwitters fell on the floor, convulsed with laughter; he'd been ragging me the whole time about still being into looking pretty, wearing hose in the subtropical heat, a different dress every day, about my middle-class values and careful table manners.

I wasn't quite playing Miz Lady anymore, but I was still a mother and a college professor's wife, and deep into the dress-and-girdle life.

I began to reexamine everything.

Communism. I was a child of the fifties and an Army brat as well. In our household, communism and child molestation were thought of in the same light. Yet most of my friends in Baton Rouge considered themselves a part of the New Left—what was the difference? Were they communists? It sounded rather like it to me. But they were lovely human beings—I respected, admired, and enjoyed them. How was that possible?

As they talked—about Vietnam, draft resistance, how the economic system was structured; Chicago; the black movement, the youth movement, and most of all, the new women's movement—firecrackers went off in my head. I didn't always agree with everything they said, but at times I felt an immediate, deep-seated endorsement. Firecrackers. "Ah-ha's," we called them.

All these people were PhD's, established scholars with a string of honors. They published articles. They even *wrote books*. And they accepted *me*. We were like partisans in a war—joined by intense camaraderie.

I wrote John only one letter that summer.

I began a journal, a place where I could record and try to distill the maelstrom of my mind. The first entries were observations about Schwitters, Colson, and O'Brien. "They seem to me no less than a different race of people. Each has an inner coherence, his own style—and in common, an acute sense that the person is political; a disregard for what other people think about him; a concern for quality—not only of his own life but those of his children, his wife, his students; a capacity to explore tenaciously what is *real*; a commitment to change. Everyone in Emporia suddenly seems the same, flat, pale, as if they'd all contrived *not* to stand out but to be invisible."

I had tried to talk to my friends in Emporia about those radical feelings that, half-formed, lived deep inside me; I had sat around in Emporia, introspective and full of self-doubt, thinking of all those things I now could say, ideas John and everyone I worked with would ignore or make light of—but which these people not only solicited from me but welcomed and encouraged.

I could feel my brain stretching, growing. *I* was growing enormously, every day.

And best of all, I was not learning from others so much as *thinking for myself*—with a mind that didn't seem so fragile anymore. They, and the total intellectual stimulation of the pressure cooker we were in, were only the catalysts.

*Spoiled, willful, and rebellious?*

Had I really been that? Or was I desperately misplaced, and struggling any way I could find to open up my life and make that magical grand connection?

I reexamined how I was living my life. Emporia. It was not enough, not nearly enough. Not anymore.

Then suddenly I was frightened.

I could feel, with absolute surety, that I was being alienated from the kind of life I had always lived, that Emporia and John and my friends would never be the same for me.

*And Kathleen?*

I could not think about her yet. I could not stop to plan. All my life, somewhere inside me I had wanted an intellectual life as intensely exciting as the one I was living. I had taken some false roads, and no roads; I had thought there was, at my age, little chance to change, to find. R. D. Laing speaks of "authentic meetings" and dialogues: I was in the midst of one, with an affinity to these people stronger than anything I had ever known.

I was scared.

But to turn from what I'd found would be to turn from *myself*—perhaps for the last time. I could not do it. I was suddenly no longer that fragile southern belle from Hamilton, Texas. I had tools now, and I would use them, if necessary, to protect what I was becoming.

I remember, near the end, the day Hurricane Carla hit Baton Rouge and everything was battened and boarded up, how we all sat out on the balcony of O'Brien's apartment and watched the wind rage. I thought of all the young blacks who must have thought they couldn't become artists, who couldn't go to the right kind of schools, who never had any encouragement, who would never make it over the hurdles.

Thinking back on Tessie and my parents and San Antonio and much more, I knew the same was true of women. That was a big Ah-ha. *Women* were the real niggers.

The wind raged through my brain. Some strange conjunction of the planets had changed my life. I knew it.

No, nothing violent happened to my body at Baton Rouge. I made my way back to Emporia in late August, to the big white house on Sherwood Way, to John and to Kathleen.

Only I didn't return.

# Four

## Cutting Loose

# 12

## "Living Lonesome"

I came back from Baton Rouge emotionally exhausted but intellectually keyed to the highest pitch. Absolutely full. About to burst. With twelve reading lists. Something important had happened to me and my first impulse was to share it as best I could. I talked nonstop for the first two days. Until everyone got bored.

I especially tried to communicate my enthusiasm to John.

"It sounds interesting," he said mildly. "I'm glad you've gotten into this."

But when I went further, telling him about my interest in Marcuse, he said: "That's sophomoric. Nobody with the sense God gave little green apples would get involved with those idiotic notions."

They didn't seem the least bit idiotic to me. My new ideas began to affect my personal life. Appalled that I was living in such a fancy house, with a black maid, I told John: "We can't keep living like this. It's crazy. All our money, all my energy, goes to support living this bourgeois farce. We don't own this house—or all these things—they own us."

*Bourgeois? Farce?*

"We have a very good life here, Judy," he said, puzzled at my sudden outburst, the exotic rhetoric. "You've always been happy with it."

"I spend so much time and energy doing things that are stupid. Don't you see?"

"No, I don't," he said, growing irritated. "Everything's been all right up to now. How come things are suddenly so different? You used to think this was a good way to live. You liked your sports car, and having a nice house—how come you don't anymore?"

"In some ways," I said quietly, "I still do. But I'm beginning to examine it."

"And me, too?"

"I love you, John," I said, sincerely. "It's not us. It's the kind of life we're living."

I'd never argued too well with John, if I argued with him at all.

People always think he's bigger than he is. They guess he's six-three, even six-four—though he's six feet even. Perhaps it's because of his voice—deep, loud, and resonant—that carries a country mile. Or just all the psychological space he takes up. Or his baroque excesses. He never did anything halfway; it was always whole hog or nothing. When he smoked, it was two packs a day. When he quit, he quit cold turkey.

There was a terrific driving force in him. I remember his father always telling him: "You can do anything. We believe in you. *You can do anything.*" I believed he could, too. He felt an obligation to be ambitious, I think, and especially to be a successful educator, as his father had been—and he was. He was a strong, dominant man. I used to like that best about him.

But it scared me, too.

I was always aware, and afraid, of his physical presence. He never struck me; I could not even imagine that he ever would. It was something far more subtle—when I displeased him, he would move quickly away, raising his voice as he went, and I would withdraw, passive and frightened.

Beginning karate lessons late that spring defined that problem for me—my hyperawareness of the physical threat of men and my own passivity in the face of it. That was the first and hardest thing to overcome.

I came back from Baton Rouge more confident than I'd ever been in my life. There had been a lot of tough people there, and I'd learned to argue them to the ground. But I didn't want to fight with John. I loved him. I still tried to avoid the fights. I was still afraid. They were inevitable now, unavoidable. *I have to fight now*, I thought, *and if I think hard enough, I can fight and win.*

I realized something else, too. I should have been arguing with John all along; all those years. It would have been kinder, certainly a lot more honest, and it might have helped to prepare him better for what came later. Why did I find it so difficult? "You mustn't fight, baby," I could still hear my mother's voice, "you *must not* fight!"

Still, I knew I was being taken advantage of. I didn't know how long I could live with that sobering knowledge. Not anymore. I would *have* to fight, or watch myself go under.

I found in a hurry that living my changing politics was troublesome; it only got harder—more complicated. I'd been reading intensely the writings of the emerging wom-

en's movement, and much of it was questioning everything, trivial and profound, that served to define women
as women in the society. I had always been—or passed
for—a "feminine" woman by the old rules, and was having
a hard time giving up my familiar modes of coping with a
hostile, masculine environment on any other terms.

On September 25th, I wrote to Colson: "Reading Kate
Millett really messes my mind, as the local natives say. I
am not half as liberated as I thought. Also, she's destroyed
all the pleasure I used to take in Henry Miller. I *know* I'm
not ready to join WITCH, not ready to give up all the
artifice and games (hell, they're part of the arsenal and I
need my weapons—anything will serve). I have quit doing
a lot of the Uncle Tom stuff I used to do so much and so
well. But I do other, more subtle things and, damn it,
enjoy it. Sometimes I like being submissive and dependent. What are the alternatives? Oh, hell!"

Two years later I had become, in fact, a WITCH, as
well as a member of New York Radical Feminists, and all
the pookie artifices and games had been violently cast
aside. I looked back in intense embarrassment on the days
when I was dragging my feet, backing and filling, still
batting my mascara-ed eyelashes. But even more humiliat-
ing, and something I couldn't bring myself to confess for
years, was the fact that it was a bunch of *guys* who'd encouraged me to get into the movement in the first place!

I notice now that there is little in the letters or in my
journal entries for that period about John and Kathleen. I
know I spent a lot of time doing things for them; but my
relationship with them seemed to have entered a half-life
period. The structure and events of our daily living were

little changed, but they had so small a part of the new life I was leading in my head. John simply wasn't interested, and Kathleen wasn't ready and couldn't understand.

My life became my own work, my thoughts, or the letters I got and wrote almost daily. My life was invested in my mailbox. I kept living with that heightened consciousness and energy I'd found at Baton Rouge, with those same people. I continued to sleep only a scant four or five hours a night, and to get up every morning with sharp expectations. Nothing had changed in Emporia; I had changed, and so had my whole perception of the reality around me.

Even my handwriting changed that fall, an alarming and mysterious alteration that surprised me as much as everybody else.

I had been married fourteen years that July first. I had developed certain patterns in my relationship with John— patterns of affection and patterns of discourse. I kept trying hard to communicate to him what had happened to me, that a part of me, too long submerged, had flowered. But our rituals were too solid, our patterns of communication too limited. He either could not understand or I could not make him share my enthusiasms. In my letters there was freedom; in my life with John there was increasing constriction.

He had been elected president of the faculty, which was why we often co-hosted receptions with the college president, either at his house or ours. I was proud of John; I could see that he was excited about his new responsibilities, and I was happy for him. Many of the parties, which he very much liked, were held at our house, since no alcohol could be served at the president's state-property home; when alcohol had to be served, we were given an entertainment allowance and the hosting fell to us, principally to me.

I would order the flowers by phone and then drive over to the florist to pick them up; I'd make complete shopping lists and buy what was needed. A whole day would have to be set aside for getting out glasses, cleaning and running errands before one of those parties. Then, when I was all dressed up like a Miz Lady, in pretty clothes and a cheek-splitting smile, I'd think: *If Schwitters could see me now, he'd laugh his buns off.*

That dress-and-girdle life palled, but I knew it would be helpful to John, who was now, increasingly, speaking of going into college administration, possibly as a dean or college president.

As October began, I felt less and less able to play that role.

"John, I simply can't be a dean's wife or a president's wife," I said.

"You can do it," he told me, and then, when I protested, he fixed his eyes firmly on mine and said: "You just won't."

Was asking me to sacrifice my career the inevitable last step? The social demands would be too great; I knew they would. I resented that he expected me to lay everything aside for a vacuous social role, but I was still inarticulate when it came to explaining that to him.

Which was part of our problem.

"That's right," I told him timidly. "I know how to play that game. I was trained for it. But I won't." I couldn't explain why not beyond saying that it was an empty, dull, inane way to live; that I hated the thought of it. And John continued to require a proper wife.

But I was not a proper wife anymore. I was on fire. I did the best teaching and research I'd ever done. I'd never dreamed it was possible to have so much energy. Now that I had it, I wanted it all for the work I loved—and I resented having to run elaborate social functions, and go to them, to minister to John's and Kathleen's needs, to administer a household.

Was there something wrong with me?

Was it possible I really did *not* find satisfaction in being a wife, a mother? No one else I'd ever known or heard about had thought or felt the way I was feeling. *I love John, I love Kathleen*, I thought; *I love them with all my heart.* But they stood between me and so much more these days. I had taken on the obligation of a marriage, and a child, willingly—but there are other life styles. *People get divorced; people die; the world doesn't come to an end.*

I had a staggering number of projects that fall, and tried desperately to fit them into an extremely tight schedule. There were those twelve bibliographies of books and essays I wanted to read; daily, the letters I received suggested more. I honed my book prospectus on black art in America, applied for grants; I rose at the crack of dawn, did my exercises, fixed breakfast, fed the cats, got Kathleen off to school. Then I was off in my MG to Washburn, sixty miles up the turnpike. I was home in time to be with Kathleen in the afternoon and then to fix dinner, make the beds, do the day's dishes and straighten the house. When we didn't have some party to go to, I'd head for my room in the basement, where I'd read, work on my slides, grade papers, write voluminous letters, or prepare for my classes until two or three in the morning.

Kathleen was getting older and more independent, imposing differences on our relationship in her own right.

But she was around less and less, preferring the company of her friends to mine. Much of the time I was with her, I wasn't *there*. I was thinking about my book on black art, or about something O'Brien said in his last letter, or about the mountains of reading lists I wanted time for.

Always before, I had been very strict about Kathleen's manners, about the way she dressed—exactly the way my mother had been with me. I saw that I was oppressing her with out-dated notions of what she ought to be like—notions that had as little to do with reality as they did with what she wanted and needed to be herself.

We began to discuss our problems with each other.

We'd had too much trouble over clothes. Once she'd come down to breakfast with her coat on, and when I'd ask to see what she was wearing, she did a flasher number—the coat opened and closed like greased lightning—and I ordered, "Back upstairs!"

*What in the hell am I doing this for?* I thought. *I'm trying to make her into what I'm trying to escape.*

"I feel like I'm your Barbie Doll," she told me, "that you dress up and send to school so everybody will say, 'Your daughter has the cutest clothes in the sixth grade.' I don't think that's right, Mama."

Nor did I.

"If you want to go to school looking like a freak, that's okay with me," I told her. So she did, and it brought considerable flack from the teachers, objections from John.

I went regularly to church all that year, taking Kathleen, getting her prepared for her approaching confirmation. From the age of eight or nine, she had been skeptical about the whole business; magic and mystery just weren't her cup of tea. I remember how once she came back from Sunday school, where the lesson had included the parting of the Red Sea, and had asked: "Mama, do you really believe all that *junk?*"

*To Schwitters, October 3:* "My colleagues are convinced past swaying that I am a *lady*, and as such should be protected, so they waste a lot of time trying to prevent me from doing myself harm. One area of harm that seems to be emerging is anything that might get me into any kind of public argument, which could get me fired. There are more and more such areas of harm."

Controversial?

I was beginning to appear just that—and worse—to many people around me. The president didn't like the blue jeans and blue work shirt that had come to be my uniform; my brother Dick, who lived in nearby Kansas City now, was convinced I had shady reasons for wanting to make a trip East for still another convention, but was considerably confused by the fact that I usually didn't seem too particular where I went—that I just wanted to go.

One weekend, late at night when both our families were upstairs asleep, he asked me: "Judy . . . are you . . . do you have a lot of friends in the East?"

I said I did. A few.

"No, I mean a *special* friend . . ."

"Well, there's Maryann. We've been friends since fourth grade . . ."

"No, no, no . . ." he was blushing a little, "I don't mean Maryann, I don't mean that . . ."

"Then what *do* you mean? Never mind, I know." I laughed, but it made me angry too. Still, I wasn't about to get into a fight with my baby brother.

We talked for hours—Dick edging around his suspicions, never really saying what was on his mind. The more he didn't say, the clearer it became that he not only suspected I had a lover, but that this mysterious stranger was probably black. Why else would I travel so maniacally? Why else would I be so interested in black artists? There *must* be a man.

"No, there isn't anyone like that. Not at all. I simply want to do my work, it's important to me. Can't you understand that?" I pleaded with him. He wanted to believe me, but he was having a tough time doing it. Just because he wasn't hearing what he expected to hear, what he wanted to hear. How could he be so persistently wrongheaded?

*Journal entry, October 5:* "It is impossible to be direct and unphony with most people. I am getting to the point where it is increasingly difficult for me to remember that I cannot talk to everyone here (no—I can hardly talk to *anyone* anymore) the way I want to. And it makes people very nervous indeed. How can I live so lonesome?"

*Journal entry, October 7:* "Work is the only way to escape, sleep hardly happens anymore."

But work wasn't an escape.

The pressures had been building all fall; the little arguments about the house and the housework had grown to knock-down, drag-out battles.

"You've got to help me more," I told John.

He'd try. But he made the beds so poorly, if at all, that I'd get the message: *I'm going to do this so wrong and it's going to be so much trouble to get me to do it, that it would be easier to do it yourself.*

We still didn't have screaming fights, but I'd get so angry I'd storm downstairs and write for hours in my journal. It was so difficult to confront him, so defeating to us both.

"I love you, John. I love you," I told him more and more—two, three times a day. I kept telling myself I loved him.

*Housework can't be so important,* I'd tell myself.

But suddenly it was.

Suddenly the pair of shorts lying on the floor by the bed became *every* pair of shorts he'd ever dropped, every single night, for the past fourteen years.

I became enraged. I snatched them up, to take them to the dirty clothes hamper, on the way picking up his dirty socks, halfway in the middle of the floor—and then the towels on the bathroom floor. Every morning, for years and years, I'd done it. Just like that.

*Why do I have to do this?*

*Household services, sexual consortium*—just like the law says.

"I already do a hell of a lot around here—more than most husbands do."

"Well, I help you much more than most wives do. And I'm working a lot harder."

"Anne teaches nearly a full load," he argued, "and she has *two* small children."

"Maybe she wants to stay a martyr for life," I said sharply. "I don't."

If I was going to get, prepare, and serve the food, the least he could do was wash the dishes. "Look, John," I proposed, "let's *help* each other, that's all I'm asking." And if I was going to wash the clothes, would he at least agree to help gather them, so I didn't have to pick them up from all over the house? "You take the beds one week, I'll take them the next."

There was a football game on TV.

He wanted to read.

He'd get around to washing the dishes only when every dish in the house got dirty, if I didn't break down and do them before—which I did.

He'd do the beds for a day, two days, and then I'd have to do them, because when people came over they weren't going to say, "John sure keeps a messy house." It was *my* house.

It was easier to lean on Kathleen, but I resented that I had to do it, and ended by being mad at them both. Kathleen was too young to understand, I too upset to explain. Anyway, no matter what I did, her room remained a wreck. And that, too, was my responsibility.

It was deadwork, nothing-to-show-for-it work. It drained and sapped me now. It always began again the next day—all of it. I'd been fighting it for years. I'd been a slob in our first one-room apartment, maniacally fastidious in my first house: two bad solutions to one problem. Now my life was too full to put up with it; *my* time and *my* energy had become too important to me. And the solution seemed so logical: that John do his share of the silly, unimportant, insignificant, boring deadwork that he would not discuss, that was killing me—and our marriage.

"I *do* help you," he'd insist and then stalk away. "I do my goddamn share!"

Desperate and furious, I made a list of everything that had to be done in the house, and who did it. When I finished it I was appalled. It was monumental.


*JUDY*

*Supply:*
– all the groceries and household supplies

- keep track of everything that's needed
- buy it, carry it home, and put it away

*Clothing:*
- keep track of everybody's clothes
- pick up and put in the hamper all dirty clothes
- sort, wash, dry, iron, fold, put away clothes
- mend all clothes, make some of mine and Kathleen's from scratch
- shop for all three of us for clothes (John buys one suit in a blue moon; I keep him in shirts, socks, and all else)
- pick up, gather, decide what has to be sent to cleaner
- his shirts to the laundry—pick them up, deliver them myself
- put away clothes, sort them every season
- put in moth balls
- put Kathleen's clothes aside as she outgrows them

*Household equipment and furnishings:*
- choose everything
- if any repairing is necessary, arrange for that
- paint furniture
- make draperies
- help paint inside and outside of house
- take care of and maintain one of the two cars.

*Housework:*
- once a week straighten up before Orelia [the maid] comes in, otherwise no time to clean—and no one could find what she put away
- pick Orelia up, take her home
- *every day* make beds, pick up clothes, books, and pa-

pers, empty ashtrays, do all extra dishes and glasses from late snacks
- prepare meals, do dishes and pots and put them all away
- plan and serve all meals
- do all shopping and washing, change linen

*Miscellaneous errands:*
- go to post office, handle all preparations for entertainment
- remind Kathleen to clean up her room and pick up clothes
- when we go out, usually make arrangements for sitters
- every month pay all bills, write all checks
- take care of all Christmas cards, buy gifts

*Teaching*
- drive one hundred-twenty miles to Washburn and back, prepare for classes, grade papers, meet enormous assignment of advisees this year, work on book, other career and social commitments

## JOHN

- works in yard—mows it regularly, improves it constantly
- takes care of and maintains all yard equipment—lawnmower, chain saw, tools
- occasionally cooks—(I clean up)
- always carries *his* plate into kitchen after dinner
- paints the house, cleans gutters, trims trees and hedges, rakes leaves; I usually help him rake

- sometimes cuts wood for fireplace; mostly we buy it; I clean fireplaces
- usually takes baby-sitter home
- sometimes, when severely pressed, he'll suggest things he wants to eat
- teaches no more than I do, travels less, has more administrative commitments

The list was longer than I'd thought it would be. I knew there was a lot, and that I'd been complaining a lot, but everything on that list had to be done. I sat staring at it, growing madder and madder. *I can't believe I've been doing all these things.* It explained a lot.

By mid-October, that strange, disassociated feeling started; I'd had it, on and off, that year in San Antonio when I nearly lost my mind. I felt so disembodied. I couldn't really tell the difference between myself and the furniture. I felt hypersensitive to myself, to everything I touched: the clothes touching my body, the weight of my glasses, of my wristwatch. I was floating in a warm swimming pool; I lost a sense of my own skin. Was it because, as in San Antonio, I was doing what all my natural inclinations told me not to do?

But this time I had weapons, and I fought it. I would not go underground again, not in any way, not ever again.

# 13

## *What Am I Doing Here?*

The party was feloniously boring.

It must have been at Bill McGraw's house because drinks were served. The staunch Baptists in the education department were all teetotalers, and I had been to dozens of these education department parties, where the good Baptists drank not at all and most of the others made up the difference by drinking themselves into oblivion.

*I can't stand a night of this again*, I thought, as I came in with John.

I had been at Washburn all day, and after the long drive home I was bone-weary. There was Eileen Blount, who had been Kathleen's teacher, and two more faculty wives who tried to hide their shock at the mini-dress I'd worn just to harelip somebody; now they were whispering. We'd played bridge with many of these couples; I had known them for years but was little closer to them now than I'd been five years earlier. We never really *talked*; it was always superficial chitchat and gossip.

*What am I doing here?*

There was always bland, boring food, and conversation to match. It all went with the invariable sage green and beige early-American decor that often seemed to me to be one of the chief visual blights of the Midwest. The men all gathered together in a clutch and the women talked about such intensely exciting matters as the parking problem at the college, the new Ethan Allen furniture one of them had bought, draperies, food prices, and what they did last summer. I'd never felt terribly close to any of them, wondered if any of them meant anything to each other.

"I'm doing some research in black art history," I answered Alice McCabe. *Dare I hope for a real conversation?* I had a strong sense of mission about my research, and always liked to talk about it.

"Isn't that interesting," she said, and with barely a pause: "Someone told me you got a new couch."

*I have so few hours to myself. Why must I serve time at dull, dull parties like this?*

I wanted to be out of it. Why couldn't I be home—working or reading? There was so much I wanted to do.

I found it almost impossible to dredge up the necessary surface comments required. For a moment I felt that eerie floating feeling, but snapped out of it. I quit listening and thought of a Susan Sontag essay I was reading—that I'd put down late the night before and hadn't been able to find a minute to finish all day. What had she said in the Hanoi Journals? *If you can't put your life where your head (heart) is, then what you think (feel) is a fraud.*

Someone introduced me to an awful little man from Colombia, the guest of honor, who was in Emporia as part of an exchange program. I supposed I was there to be nice to him. He looked like a Mexican abortionist, and he treated me like a Tootsie Roll. I tried to be gracious, to make conversation, to do my duty, but I just couldn't seem to get the project organized. Maybe if I just smiled, I could fake my way through the evening. I tried. But my face didn't want to cooperate.

I went off to a corner, smoked three cigarettes, and didn't talk to anyone.

There was only so much time. I was getting older. I couldn't wait much longer. It would be too late. I had less patience than ever with the waste, the mediocrity, the boredom that gnawed at my brain. I'd waited so long for the fires to flame up, for my life to . . .

*"If you can't put your life . . ."*

Ethan Allen. Parking problems. Silly little men you're supposed to be polite to. Time. Time. Baptists and boozers. Time.

*". . . then what you think is a fraud."* A fraud.

I left the corner of the room and found John among the men, talking about school politics.

"It's getting late," I said. "The baby sitter has to get home."

He looked at his watch. He did not want to leave.

"Please, John. I want to go home."

When we got back to the big white house after a silent drive, I stirred up the fire in the fireplace and sat down absently on the couch. John left with the baby sitter.

The weather was growing cooler, the leaves were turning; the long Kansas winter would set in within a month. I tried to think of something O'Brien had said in a recent letter, about some book he'd been reading. I could only think of how much I'd hated—positively hated—that party. Perhaps later I'd go down to the basement and read, or go to work on next week's lectures.

John came back and joined me in front of the fire, added another log, and poured himself a drink. He began to talk about his ambitions—what he wanted to do with his life. With our lives. He said he was thinking we might go to Taos for a year, where we had friends; we could live in a trailer and he could write, as he'd wanted to do. He spoke about switching into college administration—perhaps as a dean, maybe even in a job that would lead directly to a college presidency. But he wasn't sure if that's what he really wanted to do, he said, not really wanting a reply from me.

"The party left a lot to be desired, didn't it?"

I nodded my head "yes."

"What's wrong with you?" he asked quietly. "Tired, Judy?"

I nodded again.

"Oh," he said, and continued talking about his plans.

I only half-listened. Watching the bright forks of flame dancing in the hearth, I began to get angry. Taos! Another move. Did I have *this* little control over my life? Did I have to sit calmly by while he contemplated taking me away from everything that made life tolerable for me? We had always moved when and where he wanted; he made all the important decisions concerning my life, sometimes without even consulting me. I was strapped to him. I always would be. If he wanted to take a job as dean in Tennessee or Montana or Maine, I'd have to go. For years he'd done this—unwittingly, probably for my good as well as his. He'd made me wait. Kept me on the ropes for days, weeks, over some decision that would affect me deeply, would completely change my life.

For so many years of my life I had not thought much about who I was—and not much of *what* I was, either. At long last I'd been introduced to myself, and I liked what I was becoming. But it was all still *underground*, at least here, on Sherwood Way, in Emporia. And there was just no room, no place for it here. I'd been living an artificial, superficial sort of life for too long, presenting a persona to the world that had so very little to do with who I was. I was in what Laing calls a "state of becoming"—not *there* yet, but moving, moving. Finding new facets of myself every day.

I simply could not wait any longer. I had tried, since the summer, to accommodate the differences—but I had made certain discoveries: I had come to a certain place, a certain point of becoming, and I could not—*would* not—go back.

On "down" days recently, I'd felt I couldn't continue to live, couldn't even survive the way I was. I'd become like my neighbors—turn to drink or positively lose my mind. The conflicts were simply so very great, and the tension was becoming intolerable. Going bananas was a very real fear. The floating, hypersensitive feeling was appearing with greater frequency and intensity now. I knew what that meant. I'd been there before.

*But I'm not the same. I've grown.*

I'd developed systems, and structured my life rigidly. I couldn't allow anything to pile up; if the house wasn't kept tidy, I'd never catch up. I shopped on Wednesday—every Wednesday. I left messages for Orelia on the blackboard in the kitchen—our communications center. I smiled, thinking of how for weeks, not seeing her because I'd been staying so late at Washburn on her day, I'd found "Glory!" written on the blackboard shopping list. Oh, Lord, I'd thought, she's flipped out—until I found out it was a new rug shampoo.

My life was fuller. I had filled it with work I loved, thoughts that excited me. I did not think I was *in*sane or even *un*sane this time. But it *could* happen again.

I had so little privacy. And I wanted the *right* people around me. Ideas-from-books could no longer replace ideas-from-people. I'd done tons of heavy reading in the past two months, but it was like trying to fill a teacup with a firehose: I knew I hadn't retained nearly enough. I had no one to discuss it with. Colson always said you can't read alone. I resented the people around me; I'd grown hostile, withdrawn. My language had become undiplomatic, unladylike. *I'll never be dean's-wife material.*

I watched the fire rise and leap, curling yellow and red and blue around the logs—the sparks bursting up and crackling. I looked idly around the living room—the white walls and draperies, the beautiful, carefully crafted woodwork of the mantel, the pair of drawings hanging above it, the suspicious shine on the dark furniture—*damn, Orelia has gone ape with the lemon oil again; I'll have to ration her to a pint a week.*

Then suddenly I was listening to John intently. "What I really want to do, I suppose," he said, shaking the ice in his drink, "is to go off and write . . ."

So he meant it! He wasn't just talking. Was my life going to alter that radically? Be jerked up and plunked down again in some remote hole, with no job, no friends? I was sitting around, waiting for him to make up his mind—*and the terms of my life.*

". . . but there are a couple of dean's jobs I can apply for . . ."

"*No!*"

Something had snapped. The word leaped from me. I heard myself saying: "I can't do that. None of that."

He turned and looked full face at me, questioningly.

"No," I repeated firmly. "*No.* I'm going to leave. What *I'm* going to do is—"

"Okay, why?" he said calmly, standing and beginning to pace slowly around the living room, rattling the change in his pockets. "*Why*, Judy? *What's wrong with you?*"

I could feel the force of him—his size, the resonance of his voice—press against me. He seemed to be breathing up all my air. I hesitated. My decision was a surprise to me—my words a shock. I was still in many ways a nice Episcopalian lady. I wanted time to think. He kept pacing. The room, except for the crackle of the fire, was stone silent. I saw him look at me sharply.

I said: "Because I'm going to leave." And then it poured out. I said he'd been telling me for fifteen years what we were going to do and what my life was going to be like. "I can't keep living this way, John. I feel that eighty percent of the time and effort I spend in this house is wasted. I don't have the stamina of King Kong. I have work to do—work that's very important to me—and I'm not getting it done."

"Maybe I can help more around the house," he said quietly.

"That's only part of it, John. There are so many things I want to do. Maybe it's better if I just leave for a while."

"For how long?"

"I don't know."

"Where do you want to go?"

"New York," I said. "New York—to take a doctorate at Columbia or NYU." The first time I'd visited New York I'd felt I was home. And because I didn't have a doctorate, hadn't gone to a prestigious college, I was convinced I needed a PhD more than most.

"A doctorate takes a long time," he said. "You're telling

me you want to go away for two, three years, to New York. Is that it, Judy?"

"I've got to leave, John. I want to leave. I'm taking over my life and this is the direction I'm going." I told him I was very serious about the book on black art I was working on, about becoming a real scholar. "I can't do it without the credentials, and I can't get those around here because I don't want dogshit credentials any more."

He paced back and forth for a few moments, took a long drink, and looked at me again, his face white and serious. "I don't know how we can manage that, Judy."

"*We* don't have to. Because *I'm* going to do it. I'm going to have to be by myself to do this. You've been good to me, John, but you've already proved to me in every way possible that we can't do it together."

He shook his head. I could tell he didn't want to believe what was happening. He was shaken and hurt—and he didn't know what to do. "You want to go away for *good?*"

"I really don't know," I hedged.

"What about Kathleen? Have you considered her? Where does she fit into this?"

"Yes," I said. "I've thought about Kathleen. I always do. It seems to me the best thing for Kathleen would be for her to stay with you. You have a house, a job, income—you two get along . . ."

"Well, you're not really leaving me. You're going to school. We've got to keep the family together for her sake, Judy. You understand. We'll tell her, 'Mama is going off to school again.' That's all. She's done that before."

*John, I'm leaving, for godssake. Don't you see it? I'm leaving. For good.*

"She'll understand that," he said.

"She'll be better off here," I said quietly. "She's lived

here for years, in this house. I don't know where I'll be living, it's a big city and I'll be in graduate school. What kind of life would that be for Kathleen?"

"If you *really* go," he said, "how will you take care of yourself?"

"I don't know," I said honestly. "But I can't take care of anyone else."

*He isn't saying I am being incredibly selfish to put my wants before Kathleen's needs of a stable home, a mother to raise her. He doesn't have to.*

"Look," he said suddenly, setting down his drink on a table, "It's late. We'll talk about it all tomorrow. C'mon. Let's go upstairs."

"No, John. It has to be now," I said. "All of it."

He said firmly: "This isn't like you at all, Judy. You know that. These aren't your ideas. Someone's put them in your head. You're confused and tired—that's all. Let's talk about it . . ."

"No one told me to leave," I said slowly, carefully. "No one ever suggested it to me. Yes, I do have a lot of new ideas in my head—many of them from books or other people. But they've become mine; I'm making them mine."

"And Kathleen?" he asked.

"What about Kathleen?"

He couldn't find the words.

I had already thought of taking Kathleen with me. It would not work. My life would be too irregular, working all the time. Who would take care of her? There would be problems of schooling, friends, supervision.

*I love them both*, I thought, *but I cannot live with them anymore.*

"Kathleen," John said, pacing again now, gesturing with his hand as if he were about to make a point in a classroom. "What will the effect—the *pragmatic effect*, Judy—of all this be on her? Have you thought about that? About Kathleen? About Kathleen here and you there?"

I tried to tell him I was harming her by my lack of real attention now.

"That's not the question, Judy. What will happen to her if you go away—*if* you go away?"

I was still seated on the couch, unable to move. I'd finished my drink and all the cigarettes in my pack. I didn't want to get up and get a fresh one, and I certainly didn't want to ask John to get it for me. My throat was dry. I wasn't sure I could stand.

"Kathleen, Judy."

I thought of the funny, wonderful eleven-year-old who was my daughter, my own flesh and blood.

"Kathleen . . ."

"I *must* do this thing, John, no matter what the cost."

"Don't you love her?"

"Of course I love her!"

Silence.

"You don't stop loving someone just because you've got to do something else."

Silence.

"I'm attached to her. She's my child. I'll write to her, I'll see her. I'm not going to the Amazon forever."

He rubbed his forehead.

It was not like the summers in Denton, in Baton Rouge, which had been so precious to me, where I had lived out my fantasy of the "running blues." I was leaving for good. I knew it now, and John—as he paced slowly, and kept talking in his firm, sure, unrelenting voice—knew it, too.

"When you're finished," he said, "we could find a job somewhere where both of us could work."

"It's not possible, John."

"Why can't you at least wait until Kathleen graduates from high school?" He was pleading now.

So was I. "Don't you understand? That's another six years. I feel like I've wasted so much time already, John. I'm so late doing everything. It took me six years to get my BA, four years for my master's, and thirty-three years to become an independent human being. I've got so much I want to do."

*How much of me has already been lost?* I wondered. *Is it already too late?*

He began to construct an elaborate white paper, not just for Kathleen but for everybody else in the family. The truth would simply kill everybody. I insisted it would not, but that in any event, I had to do what I must do. He agreed that I should write the book, that it would be valuable for me to go to Columbia. We talked for hours. He couldn't accept that what I planned to do was permanent. I wouldn't leave until June: I had the contract with Washburn to honor. But come June, I would be gone.

"You really want to do this thing, Judy?"

"Yes," I said. I'd made up my mind.

"What do you think is going to happen?" he asked. "Who's going to take care of us—do you think Mary Worth is going to show up?"

"No."

"The only explanation," he said in measured tones, his face white and sad now, "is that you don't love me anymore."

"That doesn't have anything to do with it! But I do."

"Well, I need you, Judy. I . . . I don't think I can . . . get along without you."

"You'll have to. You've just become dependent on me

for a lot of things—things that take so much out of me. I cannot afford to give those things anymore."

No one I knew or ever heard of in my whole life had ever said things like I was saying. I saw it then—that night—and see it now as something incredibly ruthless, especially for someone who had been brought up as I had. And something absolutely necessary.

"If you *really* loved me," he said, his voice cracking now, the pain clear on his face, "I don't think you'd feel this way."

"I owe more to myself right now than I do to you, John." I got up then and walked over to the table and got myself another pack of cigarettes. "I'm very grateful to you; if it hadn't been for you, I'd never have gotten even this far."

He laughed. Then laughed again. "Maybe I should never have sent you to school."

We both laughed. "Sure," I said, lightly. "If I'd have been kept barefoot and pregnant, in ignorance . . . Slave-holders were right when they passed a law against teaching slaves to read."

"They surely were. They knew very clearly—damned clearly—what they were doing."

I said: "But it's too late now. Because . . . I can read."

"Judy, baby, if I were a *real* man, I wouldn't let you go."

"That's craziness. What does *that* mean?"

"I don't even want to think of what it means," he said, turning dead serious again.

"What would you do? Tie me to the bed post? Lock me in a room somewhere?"

"Look. Let's don't say anything to Kathleen about this yet. Let's think about it some more. Let's talk . . ."

June was nine months off; it was still safely distant.

# 14

## The Last Christmas

There was worse to come.

John, though bitterly hurt, at least had been understanding. Others were perplexed, disapproving, threatened, even angry. And then there was always Kathleen. *How can I tell her this thing?* I thought. *How can I make it intelligible to her?* I remembered my own parents' divorce; I had been the same age as Kathleen. I had asked "why?" and been given an answer that did not, *could* not, satisfy my longing to know. *Should* I tell her? What my mother had told me may have made *her* feel better, but it certainly had not helped me.

Beginning to put it into words, to a dozen different friends and relatives, made it real to me, for the first time. A frightening—and curiously liberating—experience.

"I'm leaving here," I told my stepmother by phone. "I may have to store some stuff with you." It was *real*, there were practical decisions to be made, and I made them decisively.

"God, baby," Milly said. "I'm so sorry. I didn't have any idea you were having that kind of trouble."

"I'm not having any trouble. This is just the best thing for me to do."

"You might think you're doing the right thing now," my father said when he got on the line, "but you'll look back on it and see that it's a terrible mistake. Judy, it's easier to stay and work something out than to start all over with somebody else."

It was so hard to explain, so difficult to make people understand. Without even the ability to explain hard things, no one could believe that I could be actually *doing* them. I could scarcely believe it myself.

Maureen, a good Emporia friend, had been a kind of mother to me in many ways. She was older than I, and since we were both aware of the difference in our ages, I often asked her for advice. She was a wealthy, leisured woman, who had raised two children, kept up an active interest in art, and worked with me on projects sponsored by the Emporia Friends of Art. She was Texan, and a very good wife and mother in a way I understood—a very down-home kind of way.

I knew I'd have to tell her—tell her *something*—but I'd put it off; I'd put off telling a lot of people. It was a month after that long night in October when I finally called and said: "I really need to talk to you about something, Maureen."

She said she'd be delighted to see me—it had been too long—and I drove over to her new house beyond the country club. It was cold that day in mid-November, and I realized as I drove slowly up the hill that telling her would be like telling my mother.

I didn't want to tell her. I knew that she'd be upset. I

knew she'd say the same things to me that my mother would have said.

Maureen and her husband had been kind to us; they often took us to dinner, like parents, and often invited us to their parties. I can remember turning into their gravel drive, hesitating, and then parking along one side. I remember being so glad to see her, and feeling warm and at home when I went inside that cold day, into the living room that was decorated with the same taste my mother had always had. It was a lovely room; the couches had been especially made and everything was silk and plush and velvet.

"We really ought to get together more often, Judy," she said, hugging me and smiling.

"I know how busy you are."

"Oh, never *that* busy. Not too busy for you."

She started talking about some of the problems she was having with her youngest daughter, a teen-ager. She was somewhat worried about her—the boys she was seeing, a rebellious attitude she'd taken on in high school. While she was talking, I thought: *I cannot tell her this straight. I can't do it. I'm going to have to give her one of the white papers. I can't face telling her.*

"And her manners, Judy! Heavens. They're not nearly what they ought to be." She looked at me and knitted her brows. "But you wanted to talk to me."

"Yes," I said. "I've decided . . ."

She waited, and when I didn't continue, said: "Decided what?" She said it gently. She knew something was wrong.

I blurted out: "I've decided to go to New York and work on my PhD."

"Can you do that in the summertime?"

"No," I said slowly. "No. I can't do it in the summer. I'll have to go all the time."

"How in the world will you manage with Kathleen?"

"Well, I won't."

She looked puzzled.

I said: "I'm going to leave her with John."

"My God!" Surprise changed to shock. "You can't do that. In the first place, this is going to damage your marriage. It's going to *ruin* your marriage. And what about Kathleen? She's eleven years old. Eleven." Her face was pained now.

"I know," I said.

"She needs you worse right now than she ever will. You just really can't leave her. You can't do it."

I told her that I could. As gently as I was able, I told her I couldn't just stay and keep grinding away. I couldn't stand it for six more years.

"Oh, Judy, Judy," she said, closing her eyes, wet now with tears. "You mustn't do this thing. You can't do it. What will become of you all?"

She was crying, and trying to find the words that would bring me back to my senses. "I can't imagine that you'd do such a thing. I can't criticize you. I don't know where to begin. It's so unlike you to do this."

I told her I had to do it.

She kept crying, and she pleaded with me to reconsider. I didn't cry; I didn't dare—I was very into not crying then. I tried to tell her it would be all right, we would all manage, but she was inconsolable. When I left I knew we'd never be friends again. We rarely talked after that afternoon.

Maggie, a young art historian friend at the University of Kansas, took the news differently.

I'd taken some students to the museum in Lawrence one day that week, and while there, I called her: "I've got something to tell you."

"Well, drop by and we'll get a cup of coffee."

When we were seated, I told her bluntly: "I'm dropping out."

I knew she was seriously thinking of doing the same thing. We'd had so many talks together and with some of our students, about what we perceived as the coming revolution. To change one's life radically did not seem so bizarre in that context.

She looked at me and grinned.

"I've decided that I'm going to New York. I'm going by myself and I don't know what I'm going to do exactly but that's what I'm going to do."

She started laughing.

"Well, that's what I'm going to do!"

"Far fucking out!" she said. She mentioned Emporia's society; it was where she had grown up. She said: "I can see the faces of every one of them when they get the word. Did you tell Maureen?"

I frowned. "Yes, but I didn't tell her everything. I couldn't."

"I can dig it," she said soberly. "Well, you're not the person they think you are. You've had a lot of people fooled, including yourself, for a long, long time." She looked at me and shook her head. "You are one very *heavy* lady."

And Kathleen?

I still could not bring myself to come right out and tell her everything.

One afternoon in November I mentioned that I was going away to school in June.

"Where this time, Mama?"

"New York," I said.

"When are you coming back?"

"That's just it, Kathleen," I said slowly. "I'm not sure."

"Oh," she said. And then changed the subject: "Taking me to Girl Scouts this afternoon?"

"Yes," I said.

She saw the way I was studying her. "Don't look so sad, Mama."

I managed to muster a smile. "I'm not sad, Beano." *It will have to wait. Perhaps in the spring; she'll be a little older— I'll be a little braver. June is light years away.*

There were others to tell also, and I told them what I could.

*In the Journals, November:* "What I do now matters less than my ability to *explain* it. Cogently, quietly—without getting trapped by anger and frustration."

John decided he did not want to stay in Emporia, so before Christmas we sold the house on Sherwood Way to a local businessman; we'd vacate in January. If the house had a curse—four families had owned it, and none of them left intact—I doubt it could be fierce enough ever to affect the solidity of its new owners.

One day, not long before we moved, I woke up early and started my morning routine. I remember standing in the upstairs hall, looking toward the bedrooms and then down the stairs into the front foyer. It was a lovely house; we had painted all the downstairs ourselves, made so many plans about how we wanted it to look eventually. I realized then that, despite my notion that it really belonged to Myrna Loy, I had always felt that this was where I'd spend the rest of my days.

I remember a moment thinking, *Oh, God, it's such a shame that I'm trashing all this. I'm destroying something that is very real, very important to John and Kathleen.*

For a moment I was amazed at my ruthlessness.

*Such a shame . . .*

But my thought was not even a regret. It was a simple observation, made standing in the hallway one morning before John and Kathleen were awake. I've often had that same thought since—usually when I say goodbye to them at an airport, after a visit. *It's a shame . . . but this is the way it has to be.*

One of the first of many realizations I had that, yes, I was really doing this—and how strange it seemed—was to pack away the summer clothes. John's and Kathleen's went into the trunks as always, mine into a separate box.

Kathleen still did not know, not really, that I was packing for the last time. I watched her watching me—silent, motionless—but after a while she usually trotted off to some game or Girl Scout meeting without asking me anything. I was grateful for that. I didn't want to talk to her about my leaving, not yet; I still wasn't sure I could. I'd have to watch for the right moment.

Those possessions that were mine, I began to sell or give away. I sold my cello, and I sold the treasures my mother had collected during all her travels. Going through all the accumulations of others', I knew that each belonging, each thing—whether clothes or dishes or family pictures—had taken on the special quality of the person who had cherished it, to whom it had belonged. The Japanese believe that objects accrue a history of their own, a hidden record of the use their owners have made of them; they call it *mono no aware*.

I'd load up John's van and, with a student whose hobby was antiques, take my mother's furniture—mostly pseudo-Duncan Phyfe, which was expensive but not the real McCoy—and head off to Kansas City to see what we could get for it.

John kept some of the furniture—pieces he'd become attached to, pieces he'd need. I was sorry to part with our bedroom furniture. For so many years, as graduate students and afterward, our bedroom had been sparsely furnished with only a double bed and a pair of old Sears put-it-together-yourself chests of drawers that I painted a different color each time we moved, to match the walls. The chest I had used for years was so gummed up that to get to the bottom drawer you had to take out the top drawers first. Then Papa had given us their bedroom furniture when Mama died. There was so much of it, and it was all so huge and brand new: a king-sized bed; two big bedside tables with drawers and cabinet space; two huge chests; several mirrors. The drawers in the bureau were on plastic glides, and there was wood between each row. For the first time, though I'd never particularly liked the way the stuff looked, I had more drawer space than I could use, and it all opened and closed with ease. I didn't think that was likely ever to be the case again and I was right. But chiefly, Mama had loved that furniture and I couldn't bear to sell it, so I gave it to my mother-in-law.

I gave away all my hats and most of my clothes. My Aunt Tink and my sister-in-law Ellen got the furs and the dresses; Orelia happily carried away the hats. It was exhilarating to free myself of all of it—the props and costumes of the part I had been playing.

At the same time it was also profoundly upsetting.

All during the days and evenings spent sorting things,

deciding what to save for Kathleen, what to sell, what to give or throw away, what John and Kathleen would need for their new life without me, I had a growing awareness I couldn't shake loose: it was as though I had died.

I remembered walking into my mother's closet after her death. Standing there in the closet, with my mother's soft, sweet-smelling dresses about me, I had suddenly felt like a little girl in Abilene again as I decided what to do with her clothes.

Now I was doing the same thing for Kathleen.

I got out the large quilt box my great-grandmother Molly had built herself, and put into it all the family pictures, our wedding pictures, Kathleen's baby and school pictures; if these did not yet "belong" to Kathleen, they someday would. My mother, when we'd lived in a foreign country, had always bought native costumes; I carefully laid these into the quilt box for Kathleen, too, along with her baby shoes, old Moo the pink cow, and her crib quilt that Mama and Mam-Ma had pieced for her.

I looked through all our china and silver one afternoon. The holloware had mostly been my mother's, who collected silver; the lace tablecloths had been her pride. I packed it all away carefully for Kathleen. When I closed up the box, I knew I was closing away a part of my life.

I was a ghost disposing of my own effects.

As I sold anything, I'd add the proceeds to my small bank account. I knew that every penny I could save would be needed in New York and I was banking everything I could—an enterprise in which, for fifteen years, I'd displayed no talent whatsoever. We made very little on the house, but what came out of it we split three ways.

All my anxieties, all the pain, were recorded faithfully

in the journal. Writing it down seemed to put it away so it couldn't touch me, couldn't hurt me—and so I wouldn't risk hurting John or Kathleen with my innermost feelings.

*Mid-December:* "Vibrations of resentment, hostility from nearly everybody I have dealings with. Direct and indirect accusations of running away, being irresponsible, even from those who are nominally supportive. The Christmas spirit does not prevail."

"Arguments with John, all rather low-key, continue. I suppose I only call them arguments because we have always had so few aired differences of opinion. John asks who will do the myriad idiot tasks that keep a household running? He numbers them in the hundreds; I, who have always done them, know it's thousands. I refuse to be concerned because those things have been solely my concern for so long. (No, I do not believe Mary Worth is going to show up and take over.)"

"John getting harder to listen to, talk to. So many of our conversations end with, 'Well, I can't agree with that.' Then silence. He talked, during the drive to Kansas City today, about being so angry with me. Well, now he has a taste of what it is like to have someone else arbitrarily limit his movement, control his future. I don't mean this *vindictively*. He should now understand what my situation has been for so many years, but it's clear that he doesn't make that sort of analogy yet. I don't offer it. He taught me that the only way one learns is by figuring things out for one's self."

I knew that this Christmas was going to be hard, and as it drew nearer, the awareness that this was the last time got stronger and stronger. Christmas had always been such a special time for us all—family visits and extravagant presents, special dinners and happy stories, everybody laughing together. Now that would be all over.

I wanted very much to make this last Christmas as pleasant as possible, as much like all the others as it could be.

All through the days before Christmas, as I made the house ready and went through all the ritual preparations, I had a single concern: this *had* to be a good Christmas for Kathleen.

She helped me get out our collection of Christmas tree ornaments, some of which had been in the family since before I was born. Wherever my family had lived—in the Philippines, in Japan, Germany, Pakistan—Mama had added to it. John and I continued to add to it each year; we had special handmade decorations that friends had given us; and Kathleen had made some herself over the years. She made new ones for this season. We all loved Christmastime to be wretched excess, and the way the tree looked was no exception—the more stuff on it the merrier. Christmas for us, like Thanksgiving, had always been very traditional—the ritual spun out and tied so many webs of feeling. I had seen all these holidays in the past slowly lose their shimmer for me; like that Thanksgiving in San Antonio, they had become no more than just a lot of extra drudgery. I wanted to put all those old feelings away, and make this last time all joyful and fresh.

Orelia and I polished the silver, washed the chandeliers, and cleaned the big house on Sherwood Way until it shone like a new silver dollar. We put pine boughs on the mantel—holly, cedar, and mistletoe, and bayberry candles on every available surface, with extra helpings of the cedar, because to us, that was the smell of a Texas Christmas—when we were children. We made swags of cedar and red ribbons for the staircase, a wreath for the front door, and Kathleen made a whole crèche herself.

I tried to recapture all my old enthusiasm, but I'd catch myself standing apart, detached, thinking about what everyone else was thinking— and then I'd force myself to be part of it again. John was trying, too. We were both trying very hard.

We found just the right tree and spent a whole evening decorating it together, just as we had always done. First the lights, string after string of them; then the tree ornaments themselves. Then the candy canes, the icicles, popcorn strings, and the angel on top. We didn't stop until the limbs began to groan and one of Kathleen's packages fell off for the third time. Then we all laughed and gave up. John turned on the lights, and the Christmas tree—the Santa Claus Bush, Old Daddy used to call it—sparkled to life. Kathleen's eyes sparkled even brighter. Seeing that, John and I smiled at each other.

We ordered extra wood for the fireplaces, I bought sacks and sacks of groceries for all the company we expected. I signed and sent out all our Christmas cards, thinking, each time, of the person who would receive it, what they knew of what I was doing, what they'd think. I bought and wrapped our presents—those for Kathleen chosen with special care.

John's mother came from San Antonio, and my brother Dick and his family came from Kansas City. Ellen was there with her son and a few of our old friends who were living close by.

I cooked a feast, just like always, and we all sat down to it, trying, all of us, to be as festive as we'd been in the past. Christmas had lost some of its magic for us all in recent years as Mama and John's father—two people who enjoyed it more than any of the rest of us—had died. Now Kathleen's excitement and anticipation were the only fun left in it for me.

"Oh, Mama!" she said when she saw her present—the canopy bed she'd longed for, and didn't expect.

The tree—ridiculously festooned—the big dinner, the family all sitting around our fireplace: it *was* a good Christmas, I knew it was. Kathleen was older this year but she still enjoyed it to the hilt. She was out in the snow playing with her cousins, then back inside again, warming herself, chattering away, ruining her dinner with Christmas candy.

"I wish I could help you solve some of your problems," I heard John's mother say to him in the late afternoon.

I saw him shrug.

"All I can do is hope and pray they will smooth out. For all your sakes."

Nothing more was said about my leaving—nothing that I heard. I saw Dick and John talking together, quietly, several times—but nothing was said to me.

I tried to make it a good day for all the others, but as seemed to be the case more and more frequently, I felt removed from it all, cut off—and I deliberately held myself in iron control: the emotions, had they been dealt with directly, might well have been unmanageable.

Late that night, when I looked in on Kathleen to see that she was covered up, I found her still awake, her face radiant. She had loved the canopy bed—and the last Christmas had been a happy one for her. We looked at each other for a few moments, silently, and then she said: "I just can't quit smiling." I hugged her for a long time.

# 15

## Swan Song

One thing that began to be important to me in those days—the months of days remaining before I left everything for good—was the need for control. Control over my emotions; control over my body. If I could manage those areas more efficiently, I would gain what few women I had ever known possessed: control over my life.

My emotions, my feelings, always had been a problem. In San Antonio, my mind, unable to deal with the small world I found myself in, had played a dirty trick on me. It took over my body, called a halt to everything, like a mechanical toy with an exhausted battery. I was beginning to see a connection and I could not allow that to happen again. Control was the answer, but how to manage it, how to hold it? The tensions were multiplying and mounting, and always at their heart was the question—what about Kathleen?

All that winter I exercised a rigorous mental discipline; monitoring my mind continually for any kind of laziness, reading and contemplating with an abstract precision that filled my head and left little room for emotion.

I had come back from Baton Rouge convinced I was a different person. I cut off a good deal of my long and troublesome hair and exchanged my Neiman-Marcus dresses and suits for blue jeans. I went to work on my body, too. Partly out of my new self-respect, but partly because I knew it needed more strength and energy now than ever before. I began exercizing rigorously and regularly with a self-discipline that amazed me. When I went to my doctor for my annual checkup, I expected to be congratulated on my blooming good health. He had bad news instead.

"I don't think I like the way that Pap is going to look," he told me. And then warned me to be prepared that the results might not be too good.

My heart stopped. *I've got cancer.*

"Now there's nothing to get upset about," he assured me. "I told you last year your cervix was badly eroded. It's gotten worse, that's all. I'll call you as soon as I hear from the lab, and then we'll talk about what's to be done."

I left the office in a daze. *Cancer.* My mother had died of cancer; and then within a few years, John's father, whom I had loved so much, and his aunt who had been my mother's best friend.

Two days later, I was back in the office again. Just as he'd suspected, the lab report was disquieting; there was a slight suspicion of malignancy. "I could cauterize your cervix," the doctor told me, "but I think the best thing to do is just get rid of the whole problem with a hysterectomy—you're going to have to have one eventually, anyway." I was expecting that. The big operation. It had happened already to three of the eight women to whom I was closely related; it was beginning to happen to some of my friends. But the doctor was still talking: "Now we may have a little problem with the board . . ."

"What board?" I asked.

"The hospital board. They'll have to pass on it, and they're pretty careful about women as young as you are. We'll have to get some other opinions, I've got the forms here somewhere in my desk . . ."

"Wait a minute. I don't understand."

He stopped riffling his desk drawer and looked at me. "Don't you know that after this operation, you won't be able to have any more children?"

*So, I can't have any more children.* "Yes, I know that. Of course I know that." Why did he think I'd been faithfully taking my birth control pills since a few years after Kathleen was born? "If I have to have the operation, if you say I have to have it, that ought to be the end of it."

"Well, it isn't. You'll have to see two other physicians and they will have to fill out these forms . . ." He handed me the papers.

I asked him whether men had to go through all this when they had a vasectomy.

No, that was an office procedure.

Didn't it accomplish essentially the same thing? It made them sterile, right?

Right, but he didn't have time to argue with me. Besides, what did that have to do with it? "The board considers the woman's age and the number of children she has. You are young and you have only one child."

And, oh yes, he'd have to get John's signed permission, too.

"But I'm going off to work on a PhD," I said. "I can't have any more children anyway."

He patted me on the shoulder. "Now you get on out of here, I'm busy. Be a good girl and don't worry."

I tried to be a good girl and not worry. There *was* a lot

to think about. So, I couldn't have any more children. I really didn't want any more children. Especially now. I had been relieved to see every period regardless of the fact that I took my pills without fail. I didn't trust them; didn't really trust them to work and didn't trust what else they might be doing to my body besides. Maybe, I thought, I should never have had any children in the first place. Maybe I should never have even gotten married. But neither of those possibilities had ever really existed in the world in which I grew up; I could not have imagined, at eighteen, not marrying. And if one married, one had children. There just wasn't any other way that I knew.

Life would have been so much simpler if I'd been able to accept all that, to go right on being the Miz Lady I was supposed to be. I did not, for an instant, regret that I had found someone else inside me. *But, oh, I wish to God it had all happened sooner, that I could have seen and known before I wedged my way so deeply into the lives of all these other people. Especially Kathleen.*

The hospital board met and was somehow persuaded to overlook my potential fertility. My hysterectomy was scheduled for early February.

"When you wake up," one of my student friends told me, explaining she'd had the operation a few years earlier and hadn't been prepared for the painful aftermath, "you're going to feel like someone sewed a red-hot typewriter in your pelvis—and it takes a long, long time to cool off."

She was so right.

Kathleen and John brought me to the hospital. She was too young to be allowed in my room, but she was so worried about what was happening that I thought the more she saw the better she'd feel about it. So I dressed her up like a Miz Lady and passed her off as my sister. The nurses smiled and looked the other way.

When I came to after the operation, a woman I knew slightly, whose husband was on the faculty, was standing by my bedside. She'd had the same operation three days earlier and had made the effort—and soon I learned what an effort it was—to walk down the hall to me so I would know when I woke up that I would be able to move again. She knew the pain I'd be in; she wanted to assure me that I was going to be all right.

What a marvelous gesture that was. I was ready to retract all the bad things I'd ever said about faculty wives.

One by one, the Baton Rouge group checked in, too, long distance, from all over the country. I was too dopey to talk to any of them, just nodded my head when they asked if everything was okay.

Essentially it was. I had been in excellent physical condition, and I was in very good spirits. The biopsy had been fine and I knew that I would get well fast. If nothing else, the operation, painful and scary as it had been, had given me an extra measure of control. My body could not possibly get pregnant on me now.

As winter gave way to spring, I pushed myself hard to get well and regain all my strength. As soon as I was able, Kathleen and I joined a karate class. One of the first things we learned was that the mind and the body were one; that you are able to do what you *believe* you are able to do. The strenuous classes were a good outlet for my tension, which was increasing all the time.

*Late February, in the journals:* "Waiting for June, I am like a patient with a terminal disease. But what life starts after this one dies?"

"Fred, a student of mine at Washburn, suggested today that I ride with him to New York City when school is out in June, split the cost of gas. Seems like a fine idea to me. So it is beginning to take on some reality. Tonight, for the first time, I counted. *Thirteen weeks.*"

"Another pointless scene with John. Neither of us listens, and it's so clear that we've both compromised as much as we can. *I know now that I'll never be back.* I don't know exactly what I'm going *to*, but I know so clearly what I'm leaving, and know that just trying for something else, and perhaps failing, is better than this. I *must have strength* for so much work at hand, and I want so much, with all my heart, to make life pleasant around the house for the duration of this swan song. Need to recuperate from the operation first."

"Some days, like today, I'm afraid. Afraid of myself and not really knowing what I want to do with my life once it's really mine. Afraid of what I am doing to the lives of others. John says the only justification for what I'm doing (in leaving), the *only* one, will be to be successful. What does *that* mean? I will count myself successful if I *survive.*"

I had become even more deeply involved with my radical causes, and as student protest over the Vietnam war escalated, my tenuous relationship with John grew even more strained.

We were renting a small two-bedroom duplex now, on a street far more modest than posh Sherwood Way. Kathleen despised the place, was openly hostile toward it; for me it was merely a crowded waiting station that put us all in too-close-for-comfort proximity.

John and the administration at Emporia were intent on keeping the lid on student protest; I was anxious to see it blow completely off. When the rallies and meetings began,

John and I often found ourselves on a public platform together. Wearing his suit, vest, and tie, he'd counsel patience; then I'd get up, a big, bad radical, at the same microphone, in my blue jeans and the blue workshirt that now sported a big red "STRIKE!" fist stenciled on the back, and exhort everyone to be aware of what the administration and the government were trying to do to them.

John was usually very sporting about it, advising me, before a march on the capital in Topeka, to put on heavier shoes, checking my handkerchief with vinegar on it for the tear gas, my identification, the marker saying I was allergic to penicillin. He was still taking care of me. But I felt like a private in one army who'd accidentally been billetted with an enemy general.

In the midst of all that, he took me as his guest one night to an AAUP meeting. I seized the floor and denounced that organization's historic indifference to the question of equality among male and female professors. Someone mentioned bra burning, John chimed in with the clever observation that since I'd quit wearing one I got hugged more, and I banged the table, knocking over water glasses, and informed him as well as the assembly with considerable heat and volume: "No more nigger jokes!"

It seemed to me that if I were going to change the world, I'd have to start with myself. That was all I had.

Few of our friends, many of whom I had known for years, could understand either my decision to leave or why I would sit down in the middle of the intersection of the highway and Emporia's main drag with my fellow baby revolutionaries. Several thought I should see a psychiatrist, and did not hesitate to tell John and me so.

*In the journals, late March:* "Spring is here. Saw some daffodils blooming this morning. There is no escaping it—it's here. Sometimes that's hard to take because I'm really scared, deep down, of jumping off the cliff. It's getting warm, it's time to leave. Now. How can I wait *nine more weeks?* Some student friends who know pop in daily with a countdown."

The morning Kathleen was to be confirmed, we all got up quite early and, rather too silently, began to dress. On my last trip to New York, I'd bought her a special white dress; she was happily impressed with how she looked in it, with my mantilla I let her borrow for the occasion. And she seemed to treasure the prayer book of her own, just like mine, with her name in gold leaf on the front.

In the church, I was struck once again with the beauty of the liturgy, the elegance of the hymns—but somehow part of the magic of the service was fading for me. Before Communion, the bishop placed his hands on Kathleen's head, and she was confirmed.

Later, we all had breakfast with the bishop, and I could tell by the smile on Kathleen's face that the day had meant a lot to her. There was much picture-snapping, for the grandparents who could not be present. One of those pictures lives on my bookcase now.

I heard Kathleen ask Ted if she could be an acolyte.

"You know you can't," he said.

She came right back at him. "Do you think that's fair?"

"No," he allowed.

"Well, neither do I, and as far as I'm concerned, you've seen the last of me."

I had been very conscious, all through the service and the subsequent breakfast, that I was breaking the chain, breaking the charm. I felt I was leaving a hostage to a decadent culture.

How could I help but be pleased when the hostage refused to cooperate?

Relatives visited us, at times in clusters of six or seven that spring, as they'd often done in the past, and I realized, as a batch of them would leave, amid everybody's kisses and hugs, how much I'd miss these family affairs.

We were all so much the same—in what we ate, how we talked, what we talked about. All Eudora Welty, except when it became oppressive.

Then it became more like Faulkner.

I knew I could never really break away from the family—a tribal family that's southern, it's Irish, and it's Texas. I couldn't go far enough away to really divest myself of it. There *was* no place far enough to go.

I was busy with research and practical field work that spring. I went to Chicago to photograph the famous Wall of Respect; it was a risky business, since the paintings were guarded by the Blackstone Rangers, and off-limits to the eyes of white people. But I came back safely with a treasure in slides. Then I met with an unbroken streak of disappointments. First Columbia wrote that I couldn't get into Graduate Faculties because I didn't have German and Italian. *Damn. Damn.* Then the black art session of the College Art Association convention refused to accept a paper from me; I was turned down for a grant from the National Endowment for the Humanities because I didn't have the PhD; I missed getting onto a panel I wanted to be on very badly; and finally, the ultimate disappointment— on the recommendation of a militant black artist I'd tangled with before, my book proposal was turned down by the editor who had so encouraged me since December. He was persuaded to get a black to do the book instead.

The prospect was sobering: I would be going to New York stripped of every possibility. I felt again like a terminal victim of my own folly. It was less than two months before I'd leave this safe place. *Pride will be stronger than any disaster*, I thought. *But why did I wait* so damn long. *I'm so old. And so afraid.*

Something unexpected happened. Suddenly all my danger signals were alerted. John began looking in earnest for a job on the East Coast! He applied for a spot in the New York State University system. That way, he felt, we'd at least be within "striking distance" of each other; we could meet perhaps one weekend a month, even more often.

"That's not what I want!" The thought of John so close at hand threatened to destroy everything—my independence, my need to find myself. No, no, I had to have complete autonomy; I wasn't ready to bring others into my life, to visit or be visited. Not yet. I wasn't strong enough. I had not stopped loving John, but I hadn't been able to find out yet if I would be able to free myself of his domination either. I certainly did not want him to transfer East with any expectations for our relationship; I had none. In spite of his promises to change, our lives went on exactly as before. I still had to deal with constant interruptions, his nonconscious assumption that I was still his personal servant, and most debilitating of all, his subtle belittling of anything I managed to accomplish.

It seemed to me that he would never really consider me independent, and that I would never believe that I really was, unless we were divorced. I told him I thought we ought to get it over with.

"Well, I don't want a divorce," he said flatly. "You've

made these decisions that have completely messed up my life, and I think I should be entitled to make that one myself."

It was Kathleen, of course, who worried me most. But though she must have been upset, she did not show it directly. She went to school as always, and had to be nagged in the afternoons to do her homework before she went out to play or got started with some one of her endless projects. As I think back, it seemed she took on more projects that year, she was especially busy. She went to Girl Scouts—where she'd entered a manic phase, acquiring merit badges—and to her trombone lessons. She took part in an experimental theater group for children that met on Saturdays. I noticed that she often rode her bicycle back to our old neighborhood on Sherwood Way so she could play with her neighborhood friends.

On the surface, little had changed.

But now and then, for all our best efforts, the ice broke. One Sunday when Kathleen refused to go to church with me, I blurted out: "Well, in a couple of months you won't have to worry about me riding you any more."

She shut herself in her room and I was immediately sorry. We were all as tense as a piano wire.

I felt like someone who has been away for a very long time and, coming back, sees an old world with fresh eyes. The small and ordinary events that for so many years had made up the texture of our lives—the pressures and tensions and frustrations—took on a clarity they'd never had before. I could see them far more clearly now, but it was like looking through the wrong end of a telescope. They were far away.

As the countdown progressed, I went into a protective

state of shock. I was living on my own adrenalin: I was functioning at maximum efficiency—making the long drive to Washburn and back, reading and doing research at a pace that astonished me, taking care of the house, and doing the best teaching I'd ever done.

But something inside me had thrown a protective wall around my feelings. They were locked away, like some awful secret in a Faulkner story. If I ever let down my guard, shouted, allowed myself to make the kind of remark I did when Kathleen refused to go to church, allowed myself to *feel* what was happening to us all—I knew with absolute surety that I'd lose control. I'd cave in.

I remember when John's father was dying, how he knew and we knew what was happening, and how we all—long before he died—walked around his house in San Antonio already in mourning, each numb and separate in grief. We said little. We were in a state of perpetual exhaustion. We tried to alleviate the pain by separating ourselves from it. It was much the same during those last weeks together in Emporia. We kept trying to insulate ourselves from the almost unbearable emotional stress of that time; I wrote in my journals constantly, distancing myself from what was happening—and with cool detachment recorded the storms in the household and the joys of my work away from it.

"Mama, will everything be all right?" Kathleen would ask me now and then when I put her to bed. "After . . ." For she knew now, had been told in small ways, piecemeal, not all at once—knew I was leaving, going away, for more than a summer. Maybe not forever, but it was different this time. She knew that. Knew it would be longer, knew the family would not be the same.

I could only hope and pray that Kathleen would make it

through all right. I *thought* she would make it through all right. I had to believe that or I could not have left.

On those long awful drives to Washburn, racing past the prairie grass fires and the fresh green wheat, racing along at speeds that made me count the trips like Yossarian counted missions—dreading them with a fanaticism bordering on manic refusal—I tried to imagine my future. I was going to New York to make the revolution. I knew that my place in it was going to be in the women's movement. I was beginning to think that the women's movement *was* the revolution—the real one. The periodicals and articles that Schwitters and O'Brien sent me—"No More Fun and Games," pieces from the *Liberated Guardian*—made the rounds of some of my Washburn women students like a charge of electricity. We were talking together like we'd never talked to other women before. We watched each other begin to think, begin to bloom, and begin to get angry. And we watched each other, each in her own particular style, get into trouble. With husbands and sons, boyfriends and bosses, teachers and doctors. We were spitting in Ole Massa's soup—not back in the kitchen, either, but before his very eyes. He didn't like it.

I was already in enough trouble as it was. I wasn't safe to be with. I'd been doing draft counseling for quite a while, and thanks to the demonstrations, was not unknown to the Kansas Bureau of Investigation, and Lord only knew who else. A fixture in radical circles, I flattered myself that my office phone was bugged. Who knew what might come of all of it? I had fantasies about being interned, hoped if they did lock me up, it would be among old friends.

But most of all I needed to be alone. It seemed to me I was incapable of living with anyone, even Kathleen, much less of accepting responsibility for another person: the task was to see if I could even live with myself.

As the time before June shortened, Kathleen began to leave me notes with greater frequency—and urgency. Pinned to my pillow one evening:

> Dear Mama:
>
> I have a problem. I don't know who I am. I try to be kind of like the others and I try to be me. But I just turn out weird! The other day I took a good look at myself in the mirror. I then realized how sloppy and ugly I was. Please help. Love, Bean. P.S. I love you!

*Oh, my God. My God.* How could I ask her to bear this alone? The one person I loved more than anyone in the world? I knew that no rationalizations, no assurances, no *words* could ever justify her sense of loss; and while I talked to her, soothed her, comforted her, what, finally, could I say?

Except that I would stay home, turn my back on everything.

And that I could not do. If I stayed, Kathleen simply would not have a mother. I knew I would go crazy, take to pills or alcohol; that force that was inside me but not part of me, like a disease, would take over and would carry me off to some dark place.

At least in New York, Kathleen would have a mother. Physically separated, but alive and whole, concerned and caring about her.

I could see that she was beginning to understand the dimensions of what was happening. So was I. I tried to tackle the problems one by one. *The other day I took a good look at myself in the mirror*, she had written. *I realized how sloppy and ugly I was.* I thought back to the time I was Kathleen's age, eleven. I remembered looking into the mirror myself—and hating what I saw.

That crisis I'd had to weather alone, but Mama decided it was her province to educate me on The Facts of Life. She sat me down at the dining room table and gave me some soda crackers while the lecture began. It seemed about time she told me, she'd been dropping little hints for weeks. But truth to tell, my buddy Sue Ellen McAllen had already told me everything I wanted to know on the topic, and then some, at Girl Scout camp months before. Four of us sneaked out of our cabin into the woods one night, just so Sue Ellen could give us the word, and she gave it to us pretty straight.

The gist was that people make babies just like horses do. I saw absolutely no reason to question her; I knew about horses. Besides, Sue Ellen and I had exchanged blood from our chigger bites and she was honor bound not to give me any bad information.

Mama never did get as explicit as Sue Ellen had, and mostly I remembered our mutual discomfort. I just kept eating crackers nervously and wondering if she was going to get around to the horses.

She didn't.

Maybe because Mama didn't have much use for horses.

Kathleen and I had our discussion that April, and ended up by naming all the people we both knew who were doing IT, and rolling around on the floor in fits of helpless laughter. It was the thought of the president of the college that finally destroyed us both.

Yet there were moments in my own childhood when my mother had been a real comfort to me, like the time when that Navy flier I'd dated in Japan told me he was engaged, and I was genuinely glad I had Mama there to give me consolation. Someday soon Kathleen would need that kind of comfort, and where would I be?

I worried for a long time about not having *enough* anxieties about leaving her. Was that part of the shock?

Already she was going her own way—dressing and speaking as she pleased.

"Are you coming back?" Kathleen asked me bluntly one day in late March.

"Well, I just don't know," I told her. "I don't know what's going to happen to me, Bean. I don't even know what you and Daddy are going to do."

She said nothing.

"All I know is that all of our lives are changing, tremendously, and that we're going to go and do something different now. We will still be a family, we just won't do it the way other people do. And of course you know, I want you to know, that I love you, and that I always will. That's the one thing that won't ever change."

Sometimes, as we talked, she'd begin to cry.

Sometimes I would, too.

Mostly that month I'd go around vibrating like a tuning fork. As soon as I'd calm down, drop my guard, there'd be a fight. Then there would be presents and apologies, and everybody trying to make the last few weeks as pleasant and cheerful as possible.

Poor Kathleen spent much of her time in the rafters of the garage, reading—just as I'd done in my tree house in Hamilton after my parents' divorce. And then she'd sock it to me every now and then with remarks like: "I'll bet you'll be glad when you don't have to fix our dinner anymore."

And I'd start vibrating again.

In May, my friend Audrey killed herself. She took an overdose of sleeping pills. Her husband had insisted she quit her medical practice and stay home, have a baby. She tried to go along for a while but just couldn't cut it. *She died for all our sins,* I thought, *hers too. She gave up the fight. Can I ever forgive myself for being a party to my own oppression for so long? Hell, not only didn't I recognize it, I* gloried *in it!*

Audrey wasn't the only casualty that spring.

Sarah Rossi had once been a concert star who had toured all over Europe. Now she was "just a housewife." She called one afternoon in mid-May and begged me to come and see her. She sounded so close to the edge I dropped everything and went right over. She let me in and tried to settle her two small children down so that we could talk. Her hands shook as she absently picked up a broken toy and then brought us some coffee. I sat across the table from her as she fiddled with her cup and answered the children's constant questions. Then she looked at me for a long moment, her eyes full of panic.

"Judy," her voice was trembling, "I just . . . all the time, I just feel these screams building up inside my head. Screams."

She was probably the most beautiful, gifted human being in Emporia, and I couldn't bear to see her this way. Stuck in Emporia, in that house, with two little children, she was about to go nuts the way I had. I could see it. It was what I'd started to feel again in October, that night I'd told John, what I still fought with all the will I could muster, shutting out anything that might complicate my iron resolve.

"Sometimes," she said, "I think those screams are going to explode in my head all over this goddamn freshly scrubbed floor!"

She tried to laugh, but we both knew she was dead serious.

She took my hands and held them tightly. She looked at me with those wide eyes, with the fear I'd seen in Audrey's eyes and in my own, in the mirror. *"Please,"* she said. "Please tell me *how* you're able to leave."

What could I say?

It was a long painful afternoon, and when I left I couldn't help thinking: *If shitwork kills her, Louis Rossi should be shot.*

And I couldn't help thinking, too: *If I don't leave, I'll be another casualty for certain.*

One of the things I always loved best about Kansas was that the seasons, unlike those in Texas, were clear and distinct. I had watched the leaves turn that fall, from green to a blaze of yellow, crimson, orange, and then umber; they had fallen lazily in early November, soon after I told John I was leaving, and we had raked them together in the yard, under the big elm trees. Winter had been long and cold and bitter; there was so much snow upon snow that I couldn't conceive there ever would be enough sun to melt it all. By mid-May, the new year had begun to bloom, and I realized I was consciously gazing my last on all things good and lovely every day—the rows of early green maize, the wheatfields, the pastures green and bright on my way to Washburn; my office there, with its old typewriter and racks of slides opening into my classroom; entering Emporia on the way home, with its budding elm trees peacefully lining every street, the lawns green, familiar people in front of their houses. Order and safety. Passing the old house on Sherwood Way—thinking of the Fourth of July parties we held on the lawn, while firecrackers lit up the sky over the country club. How Kathleen loved to see them—spreading patterns and color against the black sky. *Remember.*

*May 17:* "May is really better. April *was* the cruelest month."

*May 18:* "My move to New York is spawning a strange fancy—Fame and Fortune. Everybody now thinks I am going to become rich and famous, but nobody can tell me how this is supposed to happen. I can imagine getting a PhD someday, but poverty and obscurity are so built into this whole deal that I can't cope with this new fantasy."

I can remember a morning in late May, standing in front of John's dresser, putting away his clean socks—which I no longer bothered to mate and roll any more. On top of the dresser, looking back at me, were three me's: a picture of an eighteen-year-old bride, a twenty-five-year-old mother and child, and the me at present reflected in the mirror. We'd had another painful night, similar to many the previous week. A letter had arrived from John's mother, asking if I would like to come live in her basement and write my book there.

She was desperately trying to save the marriage.

John asked me to consider the proposal seriously, and I told him, Jesus Christ, I couldn't, not for one minute.

"My God, Judy, I love you so," he said. "Is there nothing I can say or do to make you stay?"

I shook my head "no."

"Judy, I absolutely *hate* to let you go."

"It's not easy for me, either."

"You're a different person," he said with resignation. "I don't know you like this."

*I think the only me he sees*, I thought as I looked in the mirror that morning, at the young bride and smiling mother, *are the two photographs.*

*May 23:* "The realization that I am *consciously* controlling my own fortune—for better or worse—for the first time in my life. Fantastic."

My last week in Emporia, Kansas, began with drawing up a new will.

It was not even signed when, as I was heading toward the turnpike the morning of my baroque final, a jeep with a steel-pipe A-frame in front barreled into me from behind, squashing me between it and another car. My car bent double, I banged my head against the steering wheel, and had to be fetched free with a crowbar. The car was totaled.

Could nothing go right? It had been a spring of disasters.

I had been unable to line up a single job or prospect of a job in New York. First Columbia; now I heard I was not eligible for any grants. I was acutely aware, as I withdrew my savings from the bank and converted them into a cashier's check, that this was my only financial security. It would not last long in New York. I had already given up my emotional security. I didn't believe in security anymore, didn't believe it even existed; *not* having security, not knowing what was going to happen, I persuaded myself, was the only kind of security I wanted.

I packed fifteen boxes of my books, and arranged for the Railway Express to pick them up, addressed to Jerry, an ex-student who was now an actor, in New York. He had generously offered me his couch until I could find a place of my own.

I packed a straw trunk with some bedding, my minimal

wardrobe, and a few dishes. I took my mother's eight-eenth-century Imari plate and nest of bowls and wrapped them in a blanket so that I could carry them in my lap. Wrapping them reminded me of all those times when I was a little girl, the way I'd packed my doll's trunk with doll clothes and then run away from home. I never took the doll, only her clothes. I'd get as far as the corner and then turn back and go home. The Imari made about as much sense as the doll clothes. *Oh, well, I can always hock it if things get really bad.* And it would serve to remind me that I had once lived in another life.

My students, whom I had loved so much, gave me a big sendoff with a marvelous array of loony presents, includ-ing a hard-hat autographed by them all. It was hard to say goodbye to them, and harder still to say goodbye to teach-ing; I had loved the work as well as the people.

One of John's students in Emporia, who'd also studied with me—who had become a kind of disciple to us both—came over to the house despondent. He couldn't under-stand what had happened to us. He said, stiffly, that he'd not only admired us singly, but also our marriage. Before he left, his eyes wet, he told me bluntly I should have sac-rificed my life, if necessary, for John.

*May 29*: "Two days to go! The great euphoric terror is building. I feel like I'm fixing to go over the highest peak on the world's biggest roller coaster."

On May 31st, John, Kathleen, and I drove the ninety miles to Kansas City together, to spend that last night at my brother's apartment. The next day, after John and Kathleen left, I'd be picked up by Fred and we'd make the drive straight through to New York.

How odd it was that day to sit by my brother's swim-ming pool as we'd done so many times before, watching

Kathleen swim and play, drinking beer and carrying on leisurely small-talk conversations with friends of my brother and his wife. *It was just as if nothing were happening.*

John and I talked about the final arrangements. I had tried hard to straighten up not only my own affairs but those of the household as well, but inevitably there were still some loose ends. John was upset and resentful during the drive, complaining that he didn't know where things were in the house, and that there was still so much I had left for him to dispose of.

"How am I going to pack and move everything by myself when I get ready to leave Emporia?" he asked. It wasn't the real complaint, just a handy excuse for everything else.

I did not argue with him. Not any more.

That night, John and I sat up until the wee hours, talking on my brother's terrace. I was careful about what I said; John had not been above using emotional blackmail in the past, and I could not afford to render myself vulnerable. But I remember that he was worried about me— whether I could take care of myself, what a difficult city New York was. He insisted that I be very careful, and advised me to call him if I had any problems, and to come back if I wanted to change my mind.

"No," I said. "I won't change my mind."

He asked also what he was going to do, how he was going to raise a daughter by himself.

We had gone over this many times together; it wasn't a question.

"You'll have to pretend I died," I said quietly.

There is a picture of me taken the next day, the day we separated: I'm wearing old, cut-off khaki shorts, ragged around the bottom, a T-shirt, straw hat, and sandals. Beside me is my Chinese straw trunk containing my meager possessions. I look—and felt—like a Chinese missionary or a refugee from the Boxer Rebellion.

I remember walking out to the old red supervan we'd hauled so much wood in, so many Christmas trees. I helped Kathleen up the high steps and she took her seat, trying hard to smile, blinking tears, still keeping her mouth shut out of habit, to hide her braces. She looked so small, sitting on the high truck seat, her sandaled feet dangling a foot from the floorboard. I shut the door for her and she leaned out of the window, took my hand, and, squeezing it tightly, held it to her cheek. "Mama," she said, her voice breaking, "when will I see you again? Will you be glad to see me?"

I told her that I loved her very much.

Then John and I exchanged a long glance, and I kissed Kathleen one last time. It was very hard for me not to cry, but I didn't. I didn't dare. I saw Kathleen's eyes fill, brim, and spill over; she put her hand over them and lowered her head.

I turned and walked slowly back to the house. I heard the engine of the old van cough and start, and I listened to them drive away.

# Epilogue

Outside my windows, New York City's West Village hums with delivery trucks and construction noises. Every day these past weeks, as I have read through the journals I kept that last year in Emporia, and the spate of correspondence I had with the group from Baton Rouge, the familiar neighborhood sounds remind me that I am really *here* now—at home. I can look out my windows and see lower Manhattan and the huge twin uglies that are the World Trade Center. The Hudson River as it curves and broadens, the cruise ships docking and sailing. On clear days, the Statue of Liberty.

My apartment is one large room, with a waterbed, couches close to the floor with large soft pillows, a few tables, and makeshift bookcases of boards and braces. The big desk where I do my writing. Lots of books. There is one window overlooking midtown Manhattan and from that I can see the Empire State and Chrysler buildings. At night, the streets are quiet and the lights from the buildings turn my windows into postcards. I've spent long

nights with the eight copious journals and the stacks of letters—some from Schwitters and Colson, others from
O'Brien; we all still keep in touch, but their lives have
remained much the same while mine has changed radically.

My wedding pictures are on my desk now, too—and
letters from Kathleen, whose scrawled hand has changed
over the past years, from that of a child to that of a young
woman—and whose mind has changed too. The weather
is turning hot; the breeze off the river cools my room, flut-
ters the leaves of the plants and makes my hanging Japanese lantern sway. It's peaceful here. It is far from Emporia. Farther still from Hamilton, Texas.

"I hope the class in karate isn't too tough," Kathleen
writes me two weeks after I came to New York. "I know
you're tough but I don't want you getting kicked in the
fanny." And then a P.S.—"How big are the phone books?
Dad says you won't be the same when you come home. I
don't believe him!"

*She still believed I was coming back then.*

As I think of those first months after I left, and of the
letters from Kathleen, I realize how much my heart was
torn—and also how carefully, without consciously doing
it, I had insulated myself against a torn heart. But I could
not go home then—and never can. Home wasn't there
anymore; it isn't there now.

The first months in New York were hard. I lived for six
weeks in the living room of Jerry's railroad flat on
Ninth Avenue. He taught me about movie lines and E
trains, bodegas and theater freebees, and all the other
native customs. At first the culture shock was immense.
The noise. The dirt. The different languages and accents.
So many people in so little space. The streets so threaten-

ing when I walked them by myself; I worked hard on my karate lessons.

I made a last-ditch effort to enter the PhD program at Columbia, still convinced it was important to have the degree. I went to see a professor there one afternoon, and he listened while I told him about my proposed research in the political content of art. He looked again at my records, noted that the language deficiencies were correctable, and that my Graduate Record Exams scores were very high, but wished I had recommendations from someone he knew and remarked it was a pity I hadn't gone to a prestige college. Then he came back to the research I wanted to do. Clearly disapproving, he said: "I can think of no one on the faculty here who would be interested in sponsoring this sort of research."

"No one at all?" I asked.

"No one. And quite frankly," he continued, "the last thing we need in art history and archeology at this time is another radical graduate student, particularly a woman."

Well, there it was—couldn't be any clearer. Still, I was flabbergasted.

"If I were you," he told me, "I'd just forget it."

I began looking for jobs but the New York art world is tight and small, and galleries had been closing, museums laying off their professional staffs. I called a curator I knew and he managed to set up an interview for me at the Metropolitan; the man was interested in having me on the staff but he said, "Somebody will have to die first. We simply have no funds to take on more curatorial personnel." I found nothing. The incident at Columbia had shaken me, and I still felt that nagging inferiority, not having the PhD.

I tried to find the women's movement, but it was elusive, amorphous. People were away for the summer. Red-stockings, the group I'd heard of in Kansas and wanted to join, had dissolved.

I was not without friends. There were people I'd known professionally, and through various radical mischief—and there were others with whom I'd corresponded about my book on black art. Maryann, my actress friend from Texas, introduced me to some of her acquaintances, and so did my roommate.

I went to the theater a lot, to Circle in the Square and Shakespeare in the Park; I gorged myself on galleries and museums; and I saw loads of films (so few of the ones I'd wanted to see came to Emporia). And I read voraciously and wrote in my journal—it was so good just to have time to do those things and a place to do them in.

Then my luck changed. I found the apartment I now live in, and a marvelous job with the National Humanities Series, touring all over the country, presenting programs of art, music, drama, literature, and history to people who lived far away from centers of culture. The Series was enormously exciting and challenging.

It lasted for two years and, with our photographs plastered on the front page of so many small-town newspapers all over America, we were, in T. S. Eliot's phrase, "famous among the barns." I loved it all: traveling, meeting such a mind-bending variety of people, learning to face audiences—any audience, of any size or description—and figuring out on the spot how to say what I wanted to say and have them listen. And talk back. I often spoke to women's groups, and what we talked about most was our changing attitudes about ourselves. I saw myself in all those women, and marveled that I was standing in front of them, my plane ticket safely in my purse, when I could just as easily have been one of them myself. I always had the feeling I could be at any second transformed into my old self, with a house and a family to return to when the program was over.

The "leaves" in New York had their own excitement, even a wacked-out kind of glamour. I was making enough money to be able to play a lot and working hard enough to feel I deserved it. Much to my surprise, there were even men to play with—single, attractive men. I met them in karate, through my work, and through my friends. I was always surprised to find these men who were interesting and intelligent, and who would still make time and leave room for such a mean-mouthed feminist. Sometimes it took longer for the breathing room to run out than others, but I was—and am—always very wary. Even if sex isn't a problem, it isn't any solution either.

The best part of my time and energy went somewhere else—it went to other women. I finally found my place in the women's movement, and joined New York Radical Feminists. Made up of the remnants of Redstockings, their style and their theory suited me right down to the ground. They became my new family, my source of emotional support and strength.

Kathleen was always very much on my mind. I financially contributed to her support and regularly wrote her long letters. When I didn't hear from either her or John for ten or twelve days, I'd worry. They had started living a strange new life, in a different place—of which I knew nothing. What did Kathleen do every day? Who were her teachers? Who were her friends? Was she eating properly? Did she remember to take her vitamins?

Mama didn't live there any more.

Even though I was traveling all over the country and working harder than I ever had in my life—making me realize all over again how impossible it would have been to keep her with me—I managed to see Kathleen several times during those first months: twice in New Mexico, where she and John had gone to live, when I was there with the Series; and once in New York, that first summer, when she came to visit me.

I was excited and more than a little apprehensive about that first visit. I was living in a strange place, living a kind of life she'd never experienced before. *She may construct defenses against me; she may even become actively hostile.*

She did not get on particularly well with the city itself. Kathleen moves slowly—perhaps in rebellion to my speed; I often used to call her Miss Molasses Foot. In New York that first summer, people walked up the back of her heels; the elevator and subway doors slammed on her before she got all the way in; and since she rarely looked where she was going, the dog-littered sidewalks were a special hazard.

The small apartment was hot; her messy ways had not improved any, and Mama was still the cross old preoccupied nag she'd always been.

One morning I found this note pinned to my pillow:

> Dear Mama, I love you very much but sometimes I don't think you're my mother any more. I hope you understand that. You said a few months ago that you were unhappy and you never wanted me to be like that. Well, I am! I love you. Love, Your daughter (I think).

Honoring our pact to write about those things we couldn't talk about, not to hide our feelings from each other, Kathleen really let it all out. Sometimes the notes and letters were wildly funny. Sometimes they hurt, and hurt deeply.

"Dear Mama," she had written to me, soon after I left home. "Can you help me? I got the rest of my braces yesterday. And they hurt. Dad isn't helping matters any. First of all, I'm in bad moods most of the time. Dad yells *more* and *louder* than he ever has and cusses about everything (almost) . . . I cry myself to sleep almost every night. Why did you leave me?! Come home! COME HOME!"

There was a time when Kathleen thought that every problem she had in the world would disappear if I would just come home. "Happy Birthday, Mama," she wrote, when I was in Colorado with the Series. "You know something? I love you! *very much.* (How old are you?) Love, Beano. P.S. I miss you *very much.* The earrings and the candle were made by me. I made the candle at camp. The pot was made by Taos Indians. Please do me a big favor— COME HOME!! Love, Bean."

And on her twelfth birthday: "I MISS YOU! When are you going to visit!? I'm making bad grades in Spanish. What are you sending me for my birthday? I know what I really want for my birthday—YOU! (And bell bottoms.) Thanks for sending those pictures; my favorite one is the one of you laughing, but Daddy and I miss you so much that every time we look at them I start crying. Daddy almost does. I'm missing you more and more every day."

As Christmas approached, even though she knew I always made sure I would be there to celebrate it with her, she wrote: "Dear Mamacita, It's here! (December, that is.) What do you want for X-mas? I want a mini-bike, Bobby Sherman records, and most of all, YOU!! Damn.

Damn. I miss you! Sometimes I start thinking about you and I just start crying and I can't stop. I tell you, I MISS YOU!! My first menstrual period was five days long. School is okay. Oh, Ricky Nelson will be in town the 3rd thru the 6th. Is it against Women's Lib if I go?"

As the letters caught up with me in remote parts of the country—Lusk, Wyoming; Yazoo City, Mississippi; Margaretville, New York—they revealed a young girl growing into early womanhood: deep emotions playing counterpoint to her active, involved life. "Happy Mother's Day," she wrote. "Or is that against Women's Lib? I miss you an awful lot. Enclosed are pictures of David Cassidy. I hope you don't think I'm crazy to be crazy about him. Everybody else does."

I didn't. And even long-distance, and through every-chance-I-got visits, I could live through her loves for Bobby Sherman, Ricky Nelson, and David Cassidy—and as she grew older, better musicians and a real boyfriend, whose "conscious" she was raising.

Sometimes, when I've seen something I've enjoyed, I'll think: *Oh, I wish Kathleen were here, because she'd enjoy this too.* The arrangement Kathleen and I have is better than the former arrangement, but I would like to have her nearer, so that we could see each other more often. As it is, we're together as often as possible.

Now, at fifteen, Kathleen is a young woman. She is full of dreams and poetry, and is a very promising visual artist as well. She's also full of laughter and fun. And she has a poise and understanding that often leaves me breathless. Last summer, when she was here, I took her with me to a radio program some of us were doing. She sat in on a panel discussion with some of the most high-powered feminists around and held her own admirably.

I was so proud of her—and best of all, we're proud of each other.

Kathleen is deeply involved in school and her friends in San Antonio. Life for me would be insupportable back there. She respects my feelings about the place, and I respect hers.

She likes what I'm doing with my life, and so do I.

Several months ago I flew back to San Antonio. Texas had been home for all of us, always. Kansas was just where we lived. John and Kathleen had finally gone back there, to make their lives in a familiar place, close to "family." Kathleen was about to have her tonsils removed; I wanted to be there with her.

Returning, I had the distinct recollection that this place had shown me some of the most difficult times of my life—my last year in high school, the first year of my marriage, the year I got sick; my father-in-law and my mother had died and were buried there. Trips back to San Antonio always make me nervous. Bad things always seemed to save up and happen to me there.

But that's beginning to fade.

In Hamilton, the old home place, my grandparents' house, belongs to strangers now and most of my relatives have moved away or are buried in the family plot on the hill. The young people leave there and don't come back.

I see my father in Texas now and then. Except for his battered old gunchy Stetson, he is still an elegant man, with impeccable suits, a variety of fancy walking canes, and shoes you can see yourself in. He and Milly came to Oklahoma to see a Series presentation there and seemed very proud of me. Milly stands up staunchly for me always—anything I do is fine with her, even if at times it may seem a bit weird. So anything she does is fine with me, too. It's not quite that simple with Pappy, and these last few years, some of the things I've said and done prompt him to raise his voice and bang the floor with one of those fancy canes. But I have the feeling he has a respect for me he never had before.

John and I are divorced now; he wanted it that way. But we are still friends, and we enjoy our occasional visits. I say more, need to listen less. He's had some difficulty explaining it all to the world; so has Kathleen.

Before she went into the hospital for her tonsilectomy, she made arrangements for me to make a speech about feminism to her high school. I agreed, with surprise and pleasure, and went dressed up for the event. At lunch, before the big speech, one of Kathleen's friends joined us and asked: "Who's your friend?"

"That's no friend," Kathleen answered, laughing. "That's my mom."

One night in San Antonio, John and I talked about what had happened three years before. "When you came back from Baton Rouge that last summer," he said quietly, "I knew that it was all over. I listened to you tell me in detail about what had happened, and I listened to the way you were talking. I knew then that you weren't going to stay."

He had never told me that before.

"I didn't know exactly *how* you wouldn't stay," he said, talking as he always does—slowly, decisively, "but I knew that you could not stay. You'd grown up."

I remembered how we'd always made jokes about his marrying me young to raise me right. "What you always told me to do," I said, "I did all too well."

"I knew right away," he said, "that you didn't need me anymore."

We talked about that night in October when, suddenly,

I'd told him that I was leaving. He said he'd visualized my getting my PhD in art history and he'd have his doctorate in education, and then we'd both work on the same campus some place. "You'd be a distinguished scholar in your field," he said, "and I'd be the dean or the president, possibly. And we'd have this beautiful life together."

"Like your parents," I said.

He paused. "I'll never forget that last day, Judy," he said. "It was in front of your brother's house. Kathleen and I were in the van, and you came down, said goodbye, and then walked slowly back up the sidewalk right to the door. We sat there for a moment in the van. You didn't turn around. You had your head down, which was very uncharacteristic."

"I don't remember," I said, honestly.

"You opened the door and walked in, and then you closed that door behind you. You never turned back to us. We drove down the block to turn around, then back by the front of the house again. Coming past the second time, I came damned near to going back in there, Judy, and saying, 'Look, you *cannot* do this thing. You just can't. We need you. We have *got* to have you.' And then . . . well . . ."

I said nothing.

"I drove out on the interstate," he said, "back toward Emporia." He closed his eyes and rubbed his forehead. "And finally, I just couldn't drive any farther. I pulled over and I stopped. I knew you weren't coming back to us. And I cried . . . and cried . . . and cried. And Kathleen did, too."

It hurt us all. It still hurts sometimes.

It would be lovely if it had been free, but the price was steep. It would have been lovelier still had none of this been necessary. Kathleen tells me some of my family never talk about me at all. "Not ever. It's as if you died under embarrassing circumstances." I have lost the regard of a number of people I love—and I am sorry for that.

"I want you to be happy," John told me so often before I left. Can I explain now that I did not do this thing for the happiness that might come of it? I have met dozens of other women these past years who have done the same thing. We all left to find a life of our own. To do something that mattered in a larger world. To see if we could. I left to test myself. I had never felt able to operate at full capacity; I'd never felt I had enough elbow room. I needed more space, a broader canvas. Hamilton, Denton, San Antonio, Emporia. They had always made me feel claustrophobic.

But in New York, alone, unfettered, never really sure what the next year will bring, I have full responsibility for my own life, which is something I never had before. I have discovered that I can take care of it damned well.

That's a heady thing.